THE ENTREPRENEURIAL SPIRIT OF THE GREEK IMMIGRANT IN CHICAGO, ILLINOIS:

1900-1930

THE ENTREPRENEURIAL SPIRIT OF THE GREEK IMMIGRANT IN CHICAGO, ILLINOIS:

1900-1930

Alexander Rassogianis

THE ENTREPRENEURIAL SPIRIT OF THE GREEK IMMIGRANT IN CHICAGO, ILLINOIS: 1900-1930

Copyright © 2015 Alexander Rassogianis.

All rights reserved. No part of this book may be used or reproduced by any means, graphic, electronic, or mechanical, including photocopying, recording, taping or by any information storage retrieval system without the written permission of the author except in the case of brief quotations embodied in critical articles and reviews.

The views expressed in this work are solely those of the author and do not necessarily reflect the views of the publisher, and the publisher hereby disclaims any responsibility for them.

iUniverse books may be ordered through booksellers or by contacting:

iUniverse
1663 Liberty Drive
Bloomington, IN 47403
www.iuniverse.com
1-800-Authors (1-800-288-4677)

Because of the dynamic nature of the Internet, any web addresses or links contained in this book may have changed since publication and may no longer be valid. The views expressed in this work are solely those of the author and do not necessarily reflect the views of the publisher, and the publisher hereby disclaims any responsibility for them.

Any people depicted in stock imagery provided by Thinkstock are models, and such images are being used for illustrative purposes only. Certain stock imagery © Thinkstock.

ISBN: 978-1-4917-7332-1 (sc)
ISBN: 978-1-4917-7331-4 (e)

Library of Congress Control Number: 2015911919

Print information available on the last page.

iUniverse rev. date: 9/9/2015

To my grandfather, John Rassogianis:
my uncles, George Rassogianis and Alex Rassogianis:
and my father, Constantine Rassogianis.

Their wisdom, foresight, and determination to succeed
helped pave the way to a bright future in a new land.

Cover Photo:

Left to right: George Rassogianis, unknown customer, Alex Rassogianis, and Constantine Rassogianis, at the St. Louis Ice Cream Parlor, corner of 26th Street and St. Louis Avenue, Chicago, Illinois 1926.

Perseverance, secret of all triumphs

Victor Hugo

TABLE OF CONTENTS

Preface xiii

I. Conditions in the Homeland Before Emigration
and Early Stages of Settlement in Chicago 1
II. The Intelligence and Perception of the Greeks as a
Necessity for Success in Business 11
III. The Necessity of Employment as a Means of
Acquiring Capital for Business 19
IV. A Description of Various Businesses Operated by
the Greeks in Chicago 29
V. Prejudicial Sentiment Displayed Toward the Greek
Businessmen and their Community 71
VI. Conclusions 87

Selected Bibliography 93
About the Author 101

PREFACE

One of the reasons why I selected to do research on this topic was my own family history. It began with my grandfather, John Rassogianis who, together with my Uncle Alex, started a candy and ice cream business in the early 1900's on the corner of 26th Street and St. Louis Avenue on Chicago's South Side. Later, they were joined by my uncle George, who was only eighteen years old when he journeyed across the Atlantic to assist his father and older brother in 1915. All of this occurred before America's entry into the World War in 1917. My father, Constantine, served in the Greek army for approximately six years, including participation in the Balkan Wars of 1912-1913. He left his mother and sister behind in Sparta in 1924 to join his father and brothers in the family business in Chicago.

Like thousands of other Greek immigrants, they were willing to do whatever was necessary to succeed. This meant hard work and very long hours. Sometimes the income was good, and sometimes it wasn't. They were guaranteed absolutely nothing. I remember my father telling me that the landlord of the building on 26th Street would knock on their front door at 6:00 a.m. on the first day of every month to collect the rent. Most of the time, they would remain open longer than usual just to earn enough to avoid eviction.

Their hardships, like many others, were numerous. On one of his trips back to Greece, my grandfather caught pneumonia on the ship and died at the age of forty-two. My father suffered many nervous breakdowns during his life; the first one was at the end of his military service. He still managed, somehow, to play a leading role in the family business and also support a family.

Uncle Alex suffered a blow to the head during a robbery in 1942 from which he never fully recovered. It occurred late in the evening near closing time. Two men came into the store and sat at a booth not far from where he was sitting. He served them and returned to the last booth in the back to finish reading the evening paper. He read the newspaper daily and listened to the news on the radio as often as he could. He made the costly mistake of turning his back to the two men and never saw or heard their approach. The wound was so severe that he couldn't even recognize his own brothers while in the hospital. He told them they looked familiar but he wasn't quite certain of their identity.

When they brought their mother over from Greece, she suffered injuries as a result of an automobile accident. She did not recover and died shortly thereafter. She was a passenger in an auto that was part of a funeral procession. A few days later it was her funeral that friends and relatives of our family would so sadly attend.

Despite facing adversity and difficult days they never gave up. Their unity and perseverance could never be broken. It is rather difficult to imagine what it was like to work between fourteen and eighteen hours a day, seven days a week, and not really know whether you were going to succeed. To go out of business was to begin a period of despair. There was no alternative but to keep going. It was often stated among Greek immigrants that shop owners worked so many hours that they were basically "married" to the business. My uncle Alex and my uncle George lived in a back room of the store. They put in so many hours that it was not practical to live anywhere else.

I mention all of this because our family story also reflects the experiences of all those courageous individuals who took the initiative to improve their lives for the well-being of their families. The process of success is the focus of this book.

I am indebted to the twenty individuals who took the time to tell me about their stories and their experiences. They are all gone now but I will never forget the pride expressed on their faces when they took me back to the early years of the twentieth century. They were the pioneers. Future generations were able to lead more productive and less strenuous lives because of the sacrifices of the immigrants. We were the beneficiaries and the inheritors of the American dream.

CHAPTER I

CONDITIONS IN THE HOMELAND BEFORE EMIGRATION AND EARLY STAGES OF SETTLEMENT IN CHICAGO

What we have to learn, we learn by doing

Aristotle

Most of the individuals who emigrated from Greece to the United States were extremely poor, and from rural peasant stock. Being an extremely individualistic and proud people, but lacking in the basic skills and training necessary to obtain decent work in urban America, they were motivated to create jobs for themselves in order to survive. Their intention was to work at whatever menial task they could, accumulate as much capital and experience as possible, and eventually open a shop or store of their own. Their concept of success then was economic, ultimately, to achieve financial independence.

They believed the best means of accomplishing this was through business enterprise. Beginning as shoe-shine boys and street peddlers, they rapidly became the owners and operators of retail establishments, candy stores, floral shops, ice cream parlors, restaurants, and motion-picture theatres. This pattern of success prevailed in almost every city in the United States where Greek immigrants settled, particularly Chicago, which was one of their most important centers.

To better comprehend the frustrations, hardships, and the eventual success of the Greek businessmen in Chicago, it would be beneficial to examine the conditions under which they lived in Greece, and their consequent motivation to begin a new life in a different part of the world. Greece had a long history of invasion, occupation, and oppression by foreigners, especially the Turks. The people managed to endure centuries of Turkish subjection by adhering to the two basic elements of their culture, namely, language and religion. They finally gained their independence through unity and a common desire for freedom.[1]

This group cohesion was remarkable since the Greeks themselves have always been an individualistic people, torn by constant bickering, petty rivalries, and sectionalism due to the separation of towns and villages by vast mountain ranges and to their unwillingness to accept the leadership of others. It was the presence of a common enemy and the tradition of a glorious past which enabled them to unify for the preservation of their homeland.[2]

Their suffering and struggle for survival did not end with their freedom from Turkish occupation in the early 1800's. The Greek economy was often depressed, plagued with high prices, an insufficient output in manufacturing, low wages for workers, and generally a low standard of living. When compared to other countries in Europe and the western world, Greece remained an agriculturally backward nation.[3] It also suffered from industrial stagnation, or rather depression, caused partly by the failure to diversify industrially, and from an unstable, ever-changing government, which did not develop clear and progressive programs for its people.[4]

After 1890, the greatest limitation on the economy was the depressed state of the nation's major export crop, the currant. The serious and somewhat sudden disaster, coupled with the rise in prices, proved overwhelming for the population to bear. The disaster stimulated an already depressed people to seek relief elsewhere for their problems. The answer was emigration.[5]

Others found another social problem: coping with the nation's traditional dowry system, which required the possession of hard currency. It was extremely difficult to find money in Greece for the purpose of marrying off sisters and daughters. Many families often impoverished

---

[1] Henry Pratt Fairchild, Race and Nationality (New York: The Ronald Press Company, 1947), p. 54.
[2] Ibid., p. 55.
[3] Carl Wittke, We Who Built America (New York: Prentice Hall Incorporated, 1940), p. 447.
[4] Thomas Burgess, Greeks in America (Boston: Sherman, French, and Company, 1913), p. 17.
[5] Henry Pratt Fairchild, "The Causes of Emigration from Greece," Yale Review, 18 (August 1909), p. 191.

themselves to save money and, eventually, give it away to a future husband who offered marriage to one of their girls.[6]

Still another cause for leaving Greece was conscription. The majority of the Greeks loved their country and were patriotic but, nevertheless, many wanted to avoid serving long years in the military. The best way to do this was to leave for America.[7]

The first Greeks to arrive were single young men who failed to earn a living in their villages and had everything to gain by leaving for America. Later the educated and cultured elements of Greek society joined the lower classes in emigrating from their country.[8] Most intended to stay in the United States long enough to accumulate sufficient capital and return to Greece to buy land, or establish a business.[9]

Actually, Captain Nicholas Peppas, who arrived in 1857 and lived in the Kinzie Street area for fifty years, and Constantine Mitchell, a Confederate soldier taken prisoner during the Civil War, were the first Greeks to settle in Chicago. After the Great Fire an immigrant from Sparta, Christos Chakonas, liked the city so well he returned to his native town and convinced many of its residents to settle in the exciting and growing American metropolis. After many followed his advice, he became known as the "Columbus of Sparta."[10] Thus, beginning in the 1870's and culminating between 1890 and 1910, approximately three-fourths of the young men in Sparta, mostly in their twenties and early thirties, left for Chicago, as well as other regions of the world.[11] Between 1892 and 1894, they were surpassed in immigration to the United States by the young men of Tripolis, which is located in the province of Arcadia, near Sparta. The news of the exodus of thousands of young men spread to more than

---

[6] Theodore M. Constant, "Greek Immigration and its Causes," Athene VIII (Spring 1947), p. 22.
[7] Theodore Saloutos, The Greeks in the United States (Cambridge: Harvard University Press, 1964), p. 31.
[8] J. P. Xenides, The Greeks in America (New York: George H. Doran Company, 1922), p. 40.
[9] Wayne Charles Miller, A Comprehensive Bibliography for the Study of American Minorities (New York: New York University Press, 1976), p. 532.
[10] City of Chicago, Department of Development and Planning, Historic City, The Settlement of Chicago (Chicago, Illinois, 1976), p. 58.
[11] Saloutos, p. 23.

eleven other provinces in Greece, including those from the Aegean islands, and, in a short time, many of those individuals d to try their luck at success in America. The majority who left G e 1870's to the early 1900's, however, came from the Pelopon outhern Greece, which included Sparta and Tripolis.¹²

Both of these cities have produced a certain type perhaps much different than any of their countrymen. Sparta and Tripolis, both situated in highly elevated areas and surrounded by barren and rocky mountains, have produced a people who were physically strong, keen, alert, and possessing a reputation as wanderers and adventurers. It is understandable that they took the initiative in leaving their country to settle in a different and unfamiliar part of the world. They were the pioneers of the Greek accomplishment in America.¹³

They would need all those attributes of survival, for settling in the United States would be extremely difficult. Other European groups, such as the Irish, Germans, and Swedes settled in the country long before the bulk of the Greeks arrived and were better informed about general American conditions, had more occupational skills, and a closer familiarity of the English language.¹⁴

The Peloponnesian immigrants arrived with no idea of what they were going to do. They were not tradesmen, mechanics, or even farmers and, for the most part, did not speak or understand English. The odds against their survival were, to say the least, overwhelming. And yet they came.¹⁵

They preferred to settle in urban areas for obvious reasons. Chicago, for example, was a large and growing city where more opportunities existed for employment than the smaller towns could offer. Also, the immigrants would have more of an opportunity to socialize and congregate with their fellow countrymen, who in turn, could assist them in finding jobs

---

[12] Ibid., p. 29.
[13] Henry Pratt Fairchild, Greek Immigration to the United States (New Haven: Yale University Press, 1911), p. 83.
[14] Saloutos, p. 25.
[15] Ibid., p. 27.

and adjusting to urban life.[16] They soon discovered that existence in the American city was fast paced and very demanding, but they were willing to work very hard at any jobs they could find.[17]

There were many reasons why the Greeks were attracted to business. Some had the idea that after they succeeded in making money they would return home and flaunt their success to their friends and neighbors in the village. They sought to prove to those back home who had perhaps doubted them that their determination and intelligence had prevailed in making them successful in America.[18]

Others were motivated by the freedom they believed they would gain. By owning their own businesses they would be free from the domination of others. Their pride in their own ethno-religious culture simply would not tolerate anyone giving them orders or telling them what to do. Some even chose working for themselves at a lower profit, if that be the case, than working for others at higher wages.[19] George Sedares, an immigrant who arrived in Chicago in 1922 and devoted most of his life to the ice cream manufacturing business, discussed this dominating trait in the Greek character:

> We are not an ordinary people. We are progressive and ambitious. We were not satisfied merely to have something to eat everyday and get by. We wanted to accomplish things. We wanted financial independence. Pride, independence, and money--all those things go together. When somebody else tells you what to do, you lose your pride.[20]

Peter Skizas, a businessman and restaurateur, knew he wanted to open his own business when he was eighteen. His goal was never to work for anyone again and become financially independent. His reasoning for owning a

---

[16] Ibid., p. 45.
[17] Ibid., p. 46.
[18] Ibid., p. 258.
[19] Ibid., p. 259.
[20] Interview with George Sedares, Forest Park, Illinois, 5 October 1981.

business was simple: "If you work for others only they will make money. You will only make money if you work for yourself."[21]

Samuel Mallason (Mallamis), a retired lieutenant-colonel in the United States Air Force, recalled that his father, an early immigrant from Sparta, worked as a beer-wagon driver and policeman before he and his brothers opened a business of their own. They simply detested working for other people and hoped to earn more money by opening an ice cream factory. They made ice cream by hand and delivered it on their shoulders by cable car. The work became much easier when they saved enough money to buy a horse and wagon, but despite the seemingly endless hardships and strenuous work, they considered their venture worthwhile.[22]

Many of the early Greeks became peddlers who roamed the streets and alleys selling fruits and vegetables from trays and baskets that were hung around their necks. When they saved enough money, they bought pushcarts and wagons in order to increase their supply of goods and, hopefully, bring in more money. This type of work appealed to many of the Greeks for various reasons. First, to get started it did not require a great sum of money. Not knowing much English, they found it a fairly easy way to begin a business. Secondly, for the independent-minded and individualistic Greek, they were working for themselves without having anyone tell them what to do, and this was very important. Lastly, for most of them, the income was fairly decent.[23]

The fruit and vegetable peddlers were not free from problems, however, and they often had confrontations with established grocers, merchants, policemen, and even the city government. In 1904, for example, the Grocer's Association of Chicago, a collective body of established grocers and merchants who resented the presence and competition of the peddlers, voiced their protest to the city council, to prohibit the selling of goods on the streets and in the alleys, or at least, heavily tax those who did so.[24]

---

[21] Interview with Peter Skizas, Berwyn, Illinois, 29 September 1980.
[22] Interview with Samuel Mallason (Mallamis), Berwyn, Illinois, 13 October 1980.
[23] Saloutos, p. 259.
[24] Ibid., p. 260.

Many Greeks thus were prosecuted but these ordinances did not alter their determination or perseverance. They fought back and insisted they were needed to supply fresh fruit and vegetables at prices people could afford. After having won a temporary victory they not only continued their business, but also they began to seriously consider forming an association to prevent later attacks.

Peddlers were also abused by corrupt Chicago police officers who often exploited their ignorance and fear. They accused them of breaking city ordinances and thus, with a threat of prosecution, forced them to pay substantial sums of money.

The Greeks became alarmed once more when, in 1909, the twenty-five dollar-a-year fee for peddling was to be raised to two-hundred dollars. Since they had gained almost complete control of the business in certain sections of Chicago, even though other ethnic groups were also involved, they believed the change in legislation was directed specifically at them. This convinced them of the need for further protection from harassment and the most effective way of accomplishing this was by acquiring citizenship and the right to vote.[25]

While the peddler was roaming the streets selling his goods and saving as much money as possible he was already thinking about the next step in his progression, which usually involved the obtaining of a small space on a busy sidewalk. From there he could locate permanently and keep a larger stock of goods. His exposure there to the community was much better and he was usually certain it would improve his business. Also, he could devote more energy to selling his goods and improving his stand, rather than tiring himself by walking up and down the streets.

When this stage was accomplished the further advancement of business was very rapid. The merchant then sought a small store that was for rent, preferably in the same neighborhood or a better one, and established himself in a respected business. After a number of years of generating a

---

[25] Ibid., p. 261.

good income, he could usually open another store, or perhaps a chain of them, or invest in property or another business.[26]

In addition to the Greeks who began their business careers in other endeavors, the progress of the fruit and vegetable seller, from street peddler to store owner, not only helped establish the foundation of the success of the Greek businessman in Chicago and throughout America, but also helped explain the character and perception of these somewhat unique individuals.

Most of the early Greek immigrants were tough, individualistic, and hard working. The fact that they were raised in poor and remote mountain villages, where mere survival was considered an accomplishment, certainly helped form their character, personality, and individualism. During their youth they were constantly reminded, both in school and by their elders, of the glory of their country's illustrious history, which included the foundations of philosophy, mathematics, and the arts; the military genius of the Spartans, the conquests of Alexander the Great, and the fierce war for independence against the Turks.

Having been indoctrinated with these legendary facts and accomplishments for many years, they often thought of themselves as the representatives of their culture in the modern world. Their heritage became synonymous with their pride and this, in turn, reflected itself in their ambition to succeed. Since most of them were uneducated, the only means of doing this was to amass as much money as possible through business and gain the respect and admiration of the community in which they lived.[27]

---

[26] Fairchild, Greek Immigration to the United States, p. 168.
[27] Interview with Sedares.

CHAPTER II

THE INTELLIGENCE AND PERCEPTION OF THE GREEKS AS A NECESSITY FOR SUCCESS IN BUSINESS

With ordinary talent and extraordinary perseverance, all things are attainable

Thomas Foxwell Buxton

To own and operate one's own business involved more than desire, pride, and an ambition to succeed. In addition to these positive and mandatory traits, the early Greek immigrants needed to possess a certain degree of intelligence to attain the fulfillment of their dreams. The writer Mahaffy, considered an authority on both ancient and modern Greece, gave his view of the Greeks:

> They are probably as clever a people as can be found in the world, and fit for any mental work whatever. This they have proved, not only by getting into their hands all the trade of the eastern Mediterranean, but by holding their own perfectly among English merchants in England. That they will become great business and professional men in the United States there can be little doubt. They come, willing to do any kind of hard physical work, but thriftily take advantage of every opportunity for advancement.[28]

The Greek merchants in England who established themselves after 1820 actually had the foresight to expand their activities into the United States, beginning in 1846. Foremost among them were the Rhallis Brothers, who opened offices in New York and New Orleans, and were mainly exporters of such commodities as cereals, flour, crops, and cotton. Their initiative

---

[28] Heike Fenton and Melvin Hecker, The Greeks in America 1528-1977 (Dobbs Ferry, New York: Oceana Publications, 1978) p. 70.

and shrewdness influenced other international Greek merchants who, very soon afterward, established themselves in these American cities.[29] Among the most noteworthy of these commercial houses were Pavlos and Galanis, the House of Argentis, Rodocanakis and Fragoudis, and the House of Fakeris.

Their venture into the American market proved very successful and enabled them to accumulate enormous profits until the termination of the Civil War which, needless to say, had disastrous economic consequences. The economic changes which took place during the aftermath of this great conflict caused most of the Greek merchants to lose their businesses. Had they been able to survive, the course of Greek business in America would have been established long before the first influx of immigrants began in the 1880's. The new arrivals would have entered better lines of business through the guidance and protection of the commercial houses, rather than suffer through the hardships, abuse, and prejudice concomitant with the early street trades. Nevertheless, a display of intelligence, cleverness, and foresight on the part of the Greeks was apparent in America long before the majority of them arrived.[30]

Greek businessmen were not the only ones who possessed intelligent and alert minds. Greek students in Chicago schools demonstrated positive traits in learning English and other subjects in the classroom, and were usually obedient and docile in most of the schools they attended. A teacher in the adult division of the Jones School, located immediately south of the downtown Chicago business district, stated that of the 252 students enrolled for the school year 1908-09, the Greeks, who numbered eighty-one, were worthy of special mention and were found to be the brightest and quickest to learn.[31]

At Jane Addams' Hull House, which played a significant role in providing a second home to many ethnic immigrant groups, the Greeks were usually described as being intelligent and enthusiastic members in

---

[29] Theodore N. Constant, "Employment and Business of the Greeks in the U.S.," Athene, VI (Winter 1945), p. 37.
[30] Ibid., p. 38.
[31] Fenton and Hecker.

the classes, and displayed great ability in forming and managing clubs, organizations, and classes for themselves.[32]

The early Greek immigrant was not only clever and alert in beginning an enterprise of his own or with others, but he also displayed a bit of ingenuity when he chose both the location and the name of his business. He found it preferable, and obviously more profitable, to be situated not only on a busy street of a business district, but on the corner, or as close to it as possible, of a busy intersection.[33] He knew that most pedestrians would use the corner to cross the street, wait for a bus or taxi, or meet a friend. He would also gain necessary exposure to the traffic which passed by in all directions. A location adjacent to a park was also favorable because of the multitude of people who would congregate there for various activities, attractions, or for mere pleasure. Opening a business, especially a restaurant or an ice cream parlor, next to a theatre almost always guaranteed the owner of a massive crowd of patrons either before or after the show.

Many of the establishments bore the same name as that of a district or community of the city, the street they were located on, a nearby theatre, or a large park. These names were already established, known by almost everyone in the city, and the easiest to remember.[34] The following list of some of the Greek-owned businesses in Chicago in 1921 and their locations gives an indication of this:

Devon Fruit & Vegetable House	1614 Devon Avenue
Belmont Restaurant	911 Belmont Avenue
Austin Candy Shop	Located in the Austin District of the City
Dorchester Cafe	6705 Dorchester Avenue
Edgewater Fruit Market	Located in the Edgewater District of the City
Loyola Restaurant	Located near Loyola University

---

[32] Theodore Saloutos, The Greeks in America. A Student's Guide to Localized History (New York: Teachers College Press, Columbia University, 1967), p. 4.
[33] Saloutos, The Greeks in the United States, p. 259.
[34] Interview with Peter Bell (Bamboles), Oak Brook Terrace, Illinois, 16 October, 1981.

Hyde Park Hotel Cafe	Located in the Hyde Park Hotel at 1511 Hyde Park Boulevard
Senate Ice Cream Parlor	Located next to the Senate Theatre on the West Side
Ingleside Shoe Repair Shop	6248 Ingleside Avenue
Humboldt Cleaners	Located near Humboldt Park[35]

Other names chosen by Greek businessmen, although not associated with streets or districts, were also popular, commonly known, and easy to remember. Establishments bearing these names were also located in all areas of the city and in some of the suburbs. The following list gives an indication of businesses using standard names:

>Keystone Coffee Company
>Victory Clothing Company
>Universal Wholesale Candies
>Atlantic Fruit Market
>Crystal Ice Cream Parlor
>Commercial Restaurant
>Puritan Chocolate Company
>International Fruit Market
>Velvet Confectionery
>Rex Theatre
>Peoples Shoe Repair Shop
>Columbia Ice Cream Company
>Meteor Candy Company
>Temptation Chocolates[36]

Many of the Greeks who worked and struggled for many years were eager to name their businesses after themselves so there would be no mistake

---

[35] George Nickolson, Greek Directory of Chicago and Vicinity 1921-1922 (Chicago: Nickolson Brothers, 1921).
[36] Ibid.

as to who the owner was. This displayed pride in themselves and their nationality. The Petropulos Range Company, the Collias and Menegas Restaurant, and Rusetos and Company Ice Cream are examples.

Others used the names of Greek cities, characters in history or mythology, and names associated with the culture of Greece. It was common to see such names as Atlas, Kentron, Hermes, Olympia, Acropolis, and Adelphia used for names of businesses operated by Greeks. Many of the owners of these concerns were proud of their culture and wanted to flaunt the Greek names.[37]

---

[37] Ibid.

CHAPTER III

THE NECESSITY OF EMPLOYMENT AS A MEANS OF ACQUIRING CAPITAL FOR BUSINESS

The greater the difficulty, the more the glory in surmounting it.

Epicurus

Most of the early immigrants who had expectations of eventually operating their own businesses realized that they first had to work for others in order to pay for their daily living expenses, gain valuable experience, and attempt to accumulate as much money as possible. They worked in stores, plants, and factories and accepted almost any job they could find. Because Chicago was one of the leading transportation centers in the country many Greeks signed up for jobs with railroad companies and were sent out west to work as laborers.[38]

Their quest for work was difficult since the Greeks were confronted with many obstacles when applying for jobs. Their unfamiliarity of the English language posed one of the greatest problems. With the exception of scientific and medical terms that were unrelated to the daily needs of the immigrants, the Greek language did not bear any resemblance to English. Many struggled with the language problem for years, while others overcame this obstacle by either attending English classes for foreigners in the evening, or learning the language by themselves.[39]

In addition to language difficulties the Greeks had other problems which prevented many of them from acquiring jobs. The surnames of many were long and deemed unpronounceable by many of the foremen in plants and factories conducting the hiring. Most of the time they rarely made the effort in pronouncing the Greek names and often skipped over

---

[38] Phyllis Pease Chock, "The Greek-American Small Businessman: A Cultural Analysis," Journal of Anthropological Research, 37 (Spring, 1981), p. 49.
[39] Saloutos, The Greeks in America, p. 3.

them completely. One immigrant recalled standing in factory lines many times looking for work but was never called. "When we went for jobs the Greek names would be hard to pronounce so the Smiths and the Joneses always got hired. I never heard a foreman call out a Greek name and I never went back again," he said.[40]

When Greeks experienced or heard about difficulties in acquiring jobs, to avoid hardship and frustration they opened businesses of their own. Chicago had many labor problems in the period between 1900 and 1930. Many factory workers who experienced job dissatisfaction and low pay chose to strike. Many unemployed Greeks, unable to speak English and being completely ignorant of trade union activities, took advantage of the opportunity and accepted jobs in striking plants, mines, and factories. Obviously, this was vehemently resented by the strikers, who quickly labeled the Greeks as 'scabs,' a term used for men breaking strike lines. This would often be followed by abuse and physical attack. Resentment of foreign workers by Americans was intensified during times of economic crisis and was felt not only by Greeks, but other minority groups as well.[41]

One such strike occurred in the diesel shops in 1904 and the vacancies were quickly filled by a group of inexperienced Greek immigrants. There was an immediate response by organized labor and the Chicago press, both of whom criticized not only those involved, but Greeks in general. Many Greek businessmen and shopkeepers who had already felt local opposition were also affected by the incident. They criticized their own people for breaking strike lines and aggravating what had already been a delicate relationship between their own groups and the local people.

They criticized the press, not for attacking the strike-breakers, but for their condemnation of all Greeks in the city. Greek societies and community leaders, fearful of attack, urged their people to advise new immigrants concerning work, social adjustment, and behavior. A message

---

[40] Interview with James Kallas, Oak Park, Illinois, 12 September 1980.
[41] Saloutos, <u>The Greeks in America</u>, p. 4.

from the influential Greek newspaper the <u>Hellinikos Astir</u>, or <u>Greek Star</u>, exemplified the sentiment of the community leaders to their compatriots:

> Let us not repeat this blunder. Americanization is the star that will guide us to prosperity, success, and progress. Let us be part of this land of plenty and not remain predatory aliens. America opens her arms to us. Let us embrace her with love and a desire to understand her laws, and her political and social life.[42]

The <u>Atlantis</u>, a Greek-American newspaper based in New York City, emphasized that the Greeks, being mostly laborers rather than professional people, were unable to be independent and should become citizens and join labor unions.[43] But the character of the Greeks, in most instances, would not abide to conformity and the struggle for financial independence continued.

Because the Greeks were confronted with many difficulties in regard to language, technical skills, and harassment by individuals in American-owned businesses, many chose to work for other Greeks whenever it was possible. By doing this they would avoid bothersome and frustrating conflicts and could focus their energies on what was most important to them, namely, making and accumulating as much money as possible. It also gave them the opportunity to meet other Greeks and possibly form business partnerships with them. To work for others of their own nationality would offer more advantages, to say the least, than working for Americans.[44]

The more fortunate individuals were those who worked for a business that was owned by a friend, a relative, or someone who emigrated from the same village as they had. Adjustment to American life was much easier under these circumstances. Chris Billions (Billionis) arrived in Chicago in 1909 at age twelve. Before he left his home in Louka, a mountain village

---

[42] Saloutos, <u>The Greeks in the United States</u>, p. 62.
[43] Ibid., p. 68.
[44] Interview with Sedares.

near Tripolis, he was told by his parents to contact a man named Dimitri Kleoris, a former neighbor and friend, who had established himself in the grocery business on Halsted Street, near the center of Chicago's Greek community. Almost every immigrant from Louka went directly to him for work and assistance. In addition to owning a grocery store, Mr. Kleoris bought a wide variety of fruits every morning at the Water Market, a center for the sale and distribution of fruits and vegetables, and distributed them to the boys working for him. They, in turn, loaded them in their wagons and sold them in the streets and alleys of the residential neighborhoods.

Although Mr. Billions did not receive any wages for his work he was provided with food and a place to live. After working for Mr. Kleoris for approximately five years, he further enhanced his experience by working as a clerk in another grocery store owned by a Greek. Since his new employer was able to pay him every week for his services, Mr. Billions was able to save a substantial amount of money and eventually open a store of his own. The reasoning behind the final phase of his progress was very obvious to him: "As long as I knew my job well when I worked for somebody else then there was no use to work for him anymore. I could do the same work for myself."[45]

Another immigrant, John Milton (Miliotis), thought it would be better to work for other co-nationals rather than Americans, and traveled throughout the United States in order to do so. Born in 1887 in the village of Mikri Vatsa, near Corinth, he left at the youthful age of twelve to work in a shoe-repair shop owned by two of his uncles in New York City. After working there for one year he left to become a waiter in a restaurant owned by a friend of his uncle, located directly across the street from their shop. He did so because he believed he could make more money, which he succeeded in doing.

One day he was fortunate enough to serve a Greek businessman from Denver, Colorado, who was visiting New York for a few days. He was the owner of a large hotel and restaurant in downtown Denver and was highly impressed by Mr. Milton's service and personality. He offered him a job

---

[45] Interview with Chris Billions (Billionis), Stevensville, Michigan, 20 September 1981.

and told him of the possibilities of making more money. He accepted the job in Denver and after spending two years there he worked in another Greek-owned business in San Francisco before moving to Chicago, where he remained until he retired. Unlike the majority of Greek men, however, Mr. Milton was not able to become financially independent. He always made it a practice to keep only a portion of his income for living expenses and sent the remainder to his mother, father, sister, and two brothers, who were living in Greece and were very dependent on his assistance.[46]

Dimitri Stratigakes came from the province of Arcadia and shared similar experiences of working for other Greeks in many sections of the country. He worked in Greek-owned businesses in Florida, Texas, Washington, D.C., and New Jersey before he and his brothers bought a hotel in suburban Chicago, which they operated for more than thirty years.[47]

George Sedares was fortunate enough to begin his new life in America in what was considered an ideal situation for a newly-arrived immigrant. His uncle owned and operated the National Ice Cream Company, a flourishing business located near the corner of California Avenue and Harrison Street on the West Side. Mr. Sedares arrived in 1922, without any knowledge of the English language or American customs, and began working immediately, delivering ice cream throughout the city with the assistance of his six cousins. He described a typical work day:

> We started at five o'clock in the morning, putting the ice cream in cans, crushing the ice, putting salt all over it, and delivering it to the stores. We carried five and ten gallon cans to more than thirty stores a day, seven days a week. We never had a day off back in those days. It was a lot of hard work.[48]

---

[46] Interview with John Milton (Miliotis), Bloomingdale, Illinois, 27 September 1981.
[47] Interview with Dimitri Stratigakes, Berwyn, Illinois, 28 September 1981.
[48] Interview with Sedares.

Regardless of how difficult the work was he considered himself fortunate to have a job, and knowing he would be able to keep it as long as he wanted. In most cases working for Americans did not offer this kind of security.

Because most of the early immigrants worked at poor, low-paying jobs while trying to accumulate as much money as possible, they were forced to live in some of the worst sections of the city, where most of the homes and apartment buildings were unsound due to cheap construction. In most of the tenement dwellings the lighting was inadequate; ventilation was poor, and the overcrowding very dangerous.

Since the Greek colony in Chicago during the early 1900's consisted mainly of young men and boys they obviously did not enjoy the good-housekeeping and comforts that a wife, daughter, or sister could normally provide. The usual custom was for a group of males to rent a room somewhere and share the household duties on some sort of cooperative arrangement.[49] Some of the meals, which were often meager and lacking in nourishment, were cooked in their rooms, while others were eaten at various restaurants in the neighborhood.

In addition to maintaining poor eating habits most of the men were ignorant of the basic rules of hygiene and this was reflected in the way they lived. Having been accustomed to an outdoor village life in Greece, they either did not know how, or did not care, to keep their rooms clean and in decent order. The ventilation was also very poor. It was not uncommon for many of them to contract various diseases, especially tuberculosis, because of the below-average living conditions. Many of those who became ill returned to Greece.[50]

Other men who belonged to the so-called 'non-family groups' lived in barns or above feed stores, rather than apartment buildings, and had no running water facilities. Many had to take showers at public institutions, such as Hull House.[51] Most of the individuals who lived under these circumstances were fruit and vegetable peddlers, who kept their horses and

---

[49] Burgess, p. 130.
[50] Fairchild, Greek Immigration to the United States, p. 199.
[51] Interview with Kallas.

some of their belongings in the barns. In 1912 one such group, consisting of fifteen men, was observed in regard to their living conditions and general lifestyle. All were between twenty and thirty years of age, unmarried, and earning approximately ten dollars a week. Each peddler paid thirty dollars a month rent for use of the barn and the living quarters above it. Their rooms were dirty, contained no furniture, and the men slept on mattresses on the floor.[52]

Another group consisted of twenty-two men under the age of thirty and all unmarried. One of these individuals assumed the responsibility of cooking for the others and keeping the rooms clean and organized. A portion of the weekly rent money was given to him for his services.[53]

Other Greek males found lodging wherever they could and were forced to live under some of the most adverse conditions imaginable. A wealthy businessman who began working in Chicago as an immigrant laborer in 1914 gave the following observation:

> I started as a shoe-shine boy on the corner of 12th and Halsted and worked from 6:00 a.m. to 10:30 p.m. every day. My wages were one-hundred dollars a year. We lived in the basement of a building on Taylor and Halsted for one dollar a week and the only heat we had in the winter was the steam from the pipes. We hardly had enough money to eat and often paid one penny to eat bread that was sometimes five days old. We would walk everywhere because we wanted to save our car fare money.[54]

Another individual recalled his early years as an immigrant youth roaming through Chicago looking for work. At that time he had no acquaintances in the city and spent many evenings sleeping on the elevated trains and in theatres for five cents because he had nowhere to go.[55]

---

[52] Burgess, p. 134.
[53] Ibid., p. 135.
[54] Interview with George Spelson (Spirotopoulos), Oak Park, Illinois, 30 September 1980.
[55] Interview with George Stoes, Stevensville, Michigan, 21 September 1981.

The overwhelming lack of family life among the Greek immigrants during the initial stage of their settlement in Chicago in the early 1990's was due, in part, to the absence of Greek women in the city. Less than five percent of the colony was female. Although some men married American women the vast majority of them preferred to wait until they were reasonably established before they considered marriage.[56] When they reached the point where they were earning a decent income or were established in a business, they either journeyed back to Greece to get married or arranged for their future bride to come to Chicago. In most instances, Greek men married Greek women.[57]

The early laborers, for the most part, were willing to adjust to the poor and inadequate living conditions for various reasons, the most important of which was to save money to either invest or open a business. They also maintained a faithful and obligatory relationship with their relatives in Greece and demonstrated this by sending money to them whenever possible. It would be used to repair their homes, pay debts to friends or relatives, or provide dowries for their daughters or sisters. The satisfaction that came from doing this often outweighed the daily hardships they encountered.[58]

---

[56] Fairchild, Greek Immigration to the United States, p. 198.
[57] Ibid., p. 216.
[58] Ibid., p. 217.

CHAPTER IV

A DESCRIPTION OF VARIOUS BUSINESSES OPERATED BY THE GREEKS IN CHICAGO

Life grants nothing to us mortals without hard work

Horace

In discussing the businesses of the Greeks, especially during the first decade of the twentieth century, one of the most popular and profitable was the shoe-shine parlor. Many of those who opened the first establishments learned this trade in Greece, making it fairly easy to utilize their knowledge and training after settling in the United States.[59] The requirements were fairly simple when compared to other, more complex businesses. A man who was in good physical condition and possessed a strong back and a good pair of hands and was willing to work fourteen or sixteen hours a day, including weekends and holidays, found this type of business appealing. In most instances it wasn't necessary to accumulate large amounts of money to open his shop because all of the necessary equipment, including chairs and shoe-shine supplies, were available on credit.[60]

The parlors in Chicago, as well as those in the rest of the country, were generally of the same type. They were situated in small stores and contained between twelve to twenty chairs for their customers. Electric fans were used to keep the shops relatively cool during the summer months. Most of the establishments were clean and well maintained.[61]

The job of the owner during most of the day was to stand by the cash register, which was located at the entrance of the shop, and collect the money. From there he could also observe his entire operation and make

---

[59] Saloutos, The Greeks in the United States, p. 259.
[60] Ibid., p. 49.
[61] Fairchild, Greek Immigration to the United States, p. 173.

certain that everything was running smoothly. Since he really didn't trust anyone, he relegated very little authority to his employees and made it his duty to stay in his shop all, or most of the day. This manner of thinking existed among most Greeks, regardless of the type of business they owned. They were very cautious in making certain that no one would be in a position to cheat or take advantage of them.[62]

The more aggressive and alert shoe-shine parlor owners established fancy and well-equipped shops in some of the best locations in Chicago. They operated mostly in the downtown area and near busy intersections throughout the city. As was the case with many other Greek businessmen, they used the names of the buildings where they were located, a district of the city, or the name of a nearby street.[63] Many became extremely successful, opening chains of shoe-shine parlors throughout the city and suburbs.[64]

Because of their shrewd and aggressive business methods and their determination to succeed by working long hours, the Greeks soon surpassed their primary competitors, namely the Negroes and Italians.[65] The Greek shoe-shine boys were said to be more attentive toward their patrons than their Negro and Italian counterparts. Many customers who frequented different parlors preferred the Greek-owned shops because the boys gave a better shine, were more respectful toward them, and did not jabber amongst themselves in their native language, which many Americans found annoying.[66]

This type of business encountered some difficulties, especially after the First World War, when shoe-shining, in itself, became less profitable. In an effort to remedy this decline and maintain their businesses, the Greeks introduced different services in their shops to attract new customers. Their operations began to include shoe-repairing, the cleaning and pressing of clothes, hat cleaning, and the selling of items ordinarily sold in drug stores,

---

[62] Saloutos, The Greeks in the United States, p. 260.
[63] Ibid., p. 259.
[64] Ibid., p. 49.
[65] Fairchild, Greek Immigration to the United States, p. 173.
[66] Ibid., p. 173.

such as tobacco.[67] Usually, the owner assumed the responsibility of these new services and became the chief shoe-repair man and hat-cleaner. By not hiring skilled people to do these jobs, he was able to save a substantial amount of money. In another effort to preserve their businesses many moved their shops next door to pool halls, barber shops, and bowling alleys in order to be situated in areas where large numbers of men congregated.[68]

Locating young Greeks to work as shoe-shine boys was not a very difficult task for the parlor owner, especially during the early years of this business. A significant reason for this was that the majority of the recruiting was done by the padrone, or labor boss, who wrote letters to friends and relatives in Greece describing his success and position of authority in America. He offered jobs, the arrangement of transportation, guaranteed housing, and numerous other opportunities to boys with ambition and a desire to improve their lives in the United States.[69]

Greece, plagued by extreme poverty, especially in the rural mountain villages of the Peloponnesus, proved to be a perfect place for recruiting. Parents with many children, in addition to meeting the expenses of daily living, had to cope with the problem of providing dowries for their daughters and looked to their sons for assistance. A boy was considered an asset because he could begin working at an early age and contribute to the income of the family. Mothers and fathers, being more concerned with their earning power than in educating them, seldom passed up an employment opportunity.[70]

The shrewd and ambitious padrone used every means available to him in his recruiting. In an effort to establish new contacts with different families, he asked his friends and relatives in the villages to offer their services at weddings and baptisms by becoming best men and godfathers whenever possible. By accomplishing this he created a bond with a particular family and thus, made it easier for himself to be entrusted with the guidance of their sons if they came to America. Periodically, the

---

[67] Saloutos, The Greeks in the United States, p. 260.
[68] Fairchild, Greek Immigration to the United States, p. 173.
[69] Saloutos, The Greeks in the United States, p. 49.
[70] Ibid., p. 49.

padrone traveled to Greece and personally offered his services at religious ceremonies for the same purpose.[71]

Most of the agreements between the parents and the padrones were verbal; entrusting any writing that had to be done to a third person who was cognizant of the matter. In most cases the details of the commitment were not revealed to anyone who was not involved in the agreement and any evidence of it was usually impossible to obtain.

The boys were usually instructed on how to reply to questioning by American officials once they arrived on Ellis Island in New York. They were expected to deny that they had received any promise or offer of a job.

In order to bypass the age law, they either possessed false affidavits of age or stated they were to live with a relative who was awaiting their arrival.[72] When this was the case, they gave the specific name and address of a father, brother, or uncle they were to join and were allowed entrance in the country when their statements were verified through correspondence by American officials.[73]

One such case occurred in 1910 when a Greek boy stated he was to meet his father in St. Louis. When authorities in New York telegraphed him and asked for confirmation, he claimed the statements were correct and that he was expecting his son to arrive shortly. Although the boy was allowed to proceed, the suspicious officials, dissatisfied with the verification, alerted someone in St. Louis to investigate. He discovered that the man was not the father of the boy but a padrone who arranged transportation for the youth to work in one of his shoe-shine parlors.[74]

One of the most attractive American cities for a boy to begin his work experience was Chicago. It was not only a leading center for business, but its Greek community; one of the largest and fastest growing in the country, included people from almost all of the regions of Greece. Even a boy with no previous commitment for work was bound to meet someone from a village near his own, merely by spending time in the Greek community

---

[71] Ibid., p. 50.
[72] Fairchild, Greek Immigration to the United States, p. 183.
[73] Ibid., p. 184.
[74] Ibid., p. 184.

on South Halsted Street. Within a short time he would usually find a job in a shoe-shine parlor.[75]

Working in the parlors was one of the most difficult and arduous jobs a youth could have during the earlier years of immigration. Most of the boys worked approximately fifteen hours a day, usually between six o'clock in the morning until nine o'clock at night, including weekends and holidays. Very often, they were required to work longer hours during the evenings when the shop was busy.[76]

Their living quarters, located in the back of the shop or at another location provided by the padrone, were usually cramped and unclean, with only the necessary facilities being available. The sharing of one bed by two boys was common and the rooms were usually lacking in proper ventilation. The poor air, inadequate food, and long hours caused many of them to become ill with various sicknesses.[77]

The wages of the boys was dependent upon many factors, including the size of the shop they were working in, location, and the policy of the person in charge. The earnings of those who worked in Chicago parlors ranged from $80 to $250 per year, the average being between $110 and $200.[78] Their counterparts who worked in smaller, less populated cities throughout the country made an average of $100 per year.[79]

In almost all of the shops, money made by the boys from tips was turned over to the owner immediately after a shine, or at the end of the day. The usual tip was 5¢ and most boys made up to $2 per day. If they had been allowed to keep their tip money their earnings would have been much greater, but the owners used it to cover the salary or the daily living expenses of their workers. This system of tipping, coupled with an overabundant supply of cheap labor, was of paramount importance in the

---

[75] Saloutos, The Greeks in the United States, p. 51.
[76] Interview with Bell.
[77] Fairchild, Greek Immigration to the United States, p. 180.
[78] Saloutos, The Greeks in the United States, p. 54.
[79] Interview with Bell.

success of the boot-blacking business in Chicago. The same pattern was used by Greeks in most of the other cities of the country.[80]

The padrone was somewhat of a father-figure to the boys. They would seek his help or advice, not only in finding work, but also in the settlement of a dispute, or a problem arising from their ignorance of the English language. The boys were totally unfamiliar with the living and laboring conditions in their new environment and usually had no one else to turn to for guidance.[81]

Recognizing the helplessness of their workers, the padrones sought to constantly intimidate them. Peter Bell (Bambales), who came from Greece in 1910 and worked as a shoe-shine boy in Kansas City and Chicago for five years, recalled that the padrones constantly verbally harassed the boys in an effort to make them work harder:

> Sometimes the bosses would say to us that since we were not making that many tips for one day it meant that we were not doing a very good job. Otherwise you would be making more tip money. When we heard this we would always work harder because we wanted to keep our jobs.[82]

Much of the intimidation of the padrone focused on the fact that most of the boys were violators of the law, and that if any were caught by government or city officials, they could be sent to prison or back to Greece. It was illegal for a child under the age of sixteen to enter the country unless he was accompanied by one or both parents, and there were provisions in the law regarding contract laborers. The boys, being constantly reminded of these facts and preferring to remain in Chicago to work instead of being sent back home, did not discuss their situation with anyone. Nor did they complain about their hard working conditions.[83]

---

[80] Fairchild, Greek Immigration to the United States, p. 181.
[81] Ibid., p. 177.
[82] Interview with Bell.
[83] Fairchild, Greek Immigration to the United States, p. 182.

Aside from wanting to earn money, most of the workers felt obligated to maintain their part of the initial agreement until it was time for them to do something else. They felt a sense of pride in remaining faithful to their jobs and to the padrone. Most of the boys were willing to tolerate the hard work and long hours because they realized that, in the long run, they had much to gain from it. Later, they could acquire different jobs with better pay under more pleasant working conditions. Eventually, they could even be operating their own businesses. When they succeeded in accomplishing something on their own, most of them viewed their experiences in the padrone system as valuable and worthwhile, seldom exposing its methods of operation.[84]

Not all of the parlor owners used the same methods in operating their shops. Many of them had different ideas as to how to operate their businesses; this was reflected in the attitudes of those who worked for them. Constantine Assimos, who arrived in Chicago in 1916 and worked at odd jobs for many years before opening his own restaurant, recalled working for a Greek who owned six or seven shoe-shine parlors in the Chicago area. He never complained about his work and did not recall having any negative experiences. He praised the owner for his attitude toward his workers and said he would never forget him:

> He treated the boys well. They got wages and he never took their tips away. He treated them well because the boys had to be happy in order to treat the customers well. It was a business. If the boss treated them badly they would eventually leave no matter what would happen to them.[85]

In the practices used by all of the parlor owners in the Chicago metropolitan area, however, any magnanimity of the padrones was rare.

The boot-blacking trade in Chicago was not without its share of difficulties and criticisms, especially from the government, public opinion,

---

[84] Ibid., p. 183.
[85] Interview with Constantine Assimos, Chicago, Illinois 5 November 1981.

and segments of the Greek community that condemned the padrones and their business practices. The primary interest of the United States Government was that most of the boys working in the shops were in violation of the contract labor law. They hired special immigrant inspectors, usually Greeks, to investigate the conditions in the Greek communities throughout the country and report their findings.

Obviously, their attention focused on the shoe-shine parlors and other businesses which employed young boys.[86] The boys feared the inspectors and were often warned of their impending visits to the city where they were working. Peter Bell, working as a shoe-shine boy in Kansas City, Missouri in 1911, admitted that this was the reason why he left and, ultimately made his way to Chicago:

> The man's name was Mr. Daskalakis and he was very well known among the boys. They feared him because they knew they would not only be out of a job but would be sent back to Greece if they didn't have a sponsor. He would be sure to check all the shoe-shine parlors because that's where most of the boys were. When I heard he was coming, I got scared and went to several different cities before I came to Chicago.[87]

A common complaint against the padrones was that they purposely confined the boys to the shops to prevent them from attending night school classes where they could learn English and come into contact with other people. They claimed the bosses feared this because their workers would ultimately learn enough about the American way of life and eventually would not need the jobs and services provided by the padrone. Most of the parlor owners claimed that this was not the case and that their reason was simply that they could not spare the boys from the business.[88]

---

[86] Fairchild, Greek Immigration to the United States, p. 177.
[87] Interview with Bell.
[88] Fairchild, Greek Immigration to the United States, p. 180.

When many individuals in the Greek community learned about the exploitation of their youth and the shameful conduct of some of their compatriots, they became angry and embarrassed. Influential Greek newspapers, such as the Atlantis, urged its people to end the harsh conditions the boys were subjected to. The Greek press often reprinted articles from American newspapers condemning the padrone system in an effort to influence as many of their co-nationals as possible. American papers referred to the shoe-shine parlors and other businesses which employed young boys as 'flesh-emporiums.' The Atlantis was concerned about the welfare of the boys and the embarrassment and disgrace Greeks suffered as a result of the news.[89]

Because of increased pressure from the Greek and American communities, the padrones agreed to initiate improved working conditions and better pay for the boys. Daily work schedules were decreased by three or four hours, allowing the workers time to attend night classes. Even benefits such as hospitalization and sick pay were agreed upon.[90]

Despite the improvements in working conditions and greater acceptance, the shoe- shining business began to decline when confronted with other obstacles. By the mid 1920's Greek immigrants, as well as those of other ethnic groups, were more knowledgeable of the language and the customs of America and were capable of obtaining more desirable jobs with better pay, less hours, and more pleasant working conditions. Greek parlor owners who included hat and clothes cleaning as part of their businesses faced increased competition in these services, especially from Jewish immigrants.[91] Since it also became increasingly difficult to find cheap labor, many Greeks invested in other businesses which were both more respectable and did not require much help to operate.[92]

One of the most popular and important endeavors the early Greek immigrants engaged in, perfected, and eventually dominated, was the confectionery business. Its beginnings can be traced to the early street

---

[89] Saloutos, The Greeks in the United States, p. 54.
[90] "More About the Labor Meeting," Saloniki, 15 April 1916, p. 1.
[91] "Bootblacks Protective Union of Illinois," Chicago Greek Daily, 11 February 1928, p. 1.
[92] Saloutos, The Greeks in the United States, p. 56.

peddlers who sold candy and pastry and eventually operated small shops which offered these and other products, such as ice-cream. The Greek candy business, however, was started in New York City long before the majority of Greeks began emigrating to the United States in the early 1880's. It was there that Eleftherios Palalas and Panagiotis Hatziteres, who arrived in 1869 from Smyrna with the intention of manufacturing oriental pastries and various types of candies, opened the first Greek candy factory.

In 1877 Pelalas moved to Springfield, Massachusetts to manage Kibbe Brothers Candy Factory, eventually opening several candy shops of his own. Hatziteres remained in New York and expanded his operation to include two more businesses, the American Confectionery Company and the Novelty Candy Company.[93]

Ice-cream parlors, like the shoe-shine shops, did not require a large sum of money to open, and many of the individuals who entered this line first learned it in Greece.[94] Those with no experience worked in Greek-owned shops and stayed as long as was necessary to learn the business and accumulate enough money before opening stores of their own.

The first such shops in Chicago were located near Greek grocery stores, restaurants, and coffeehouses on Halsted Street, where the owners were certain to conduct business with members of their own nationality. They could also cater to large groups who were celebrating weddings, name days, baptisms, and other religious ceremonies.

The next step was to open stores in other areas of the city, especially downtown or in other busy sections where large numbers of people congregated. Favorable locations included those adjacent to movie-theatres, parks, or other places which offered public entertainment.[95]

Most of the ice-cream parlors were generally of the same type since most of the owners received their ideas while working for other Greeks. They contained small tables or booths for the customers and facilities for selling candy, ice cream, and soda water. Shops operated by wealthy

---

[93] Theodore N. Constant, "Employment and Business of the Greeks in the U.S.," Athene, VII (Summer 1946), p. 40.
[94] "Chicago--the Mecca of the Candy Business," Greek Star, 1 April 1904, p. 2.
[95] Saloutos, The Greeks in the United States, p. 262.

proprietors were more dazzling than the others and contained mirrors, fancy ornaments, and beautiful furnishings. One of the most elegant and largest in the city was located downtown on the corner of Van Buren and State Streets. The furnishings of this ornate parlor were elaborate. Most of the shops were attractive, clean, and well-maintained.[96]

The owners of the ice-cream parlors generally manufactured their own goods. They made their own candies and ice cream in the back of the store, in the basement, or in whatever other space was available to them. They were assisted by members of their own family or hired help. As was the case in most of the other businesses, the hours were long and the work very difficult. George Rassogianis, who came from Sparta and operated a candy shop with his father and two older brothers in the Lawndale district on Chicago's West Side, recalled the frustration of his daily work routine:

> During the early days there was no money. We would barely make enough to get by. I worked all day long. I couldn't count the hours I worked--probably 18 hours a day. We sold a lot of sodas for 5¢ but barely made enough money to pay the rent. We would kill ourselves just to make a nickel. I never had a happy day in America. It was only work.[97]

The hard work, devotion, and pride of the candy shop owners usually reflected itself in the type of service and the quality of food rendered to the public. The reputation of the Greek-owned ice-cream parlors in Chicago was generally favorable. This opinion was shared not only by the people who patronized these establishments but by state food commissioners, local city officials, and writers of food publications. One such publication, Purity, was dedicated to the interests of pure food and often contained a list of food-service businesses throughout the country which had violated food laws. In its listings for the year 1908, a number of leading American

---

[96] Fairchild, Greek Immigration to the United States, p. 169.
[97] Interview with George Rassogianis, Bloomingdale, Illinois, 27 September 1981.

manufacturers were discovered to be using unnatural ingredients in their candy; however, no Greek-owned establishments were named.

During the same year an investigation by state food inspectors of Greek-owned ice-cream parlors in Chicago sampled various candies from each store. The ingredients and quality of the candy, especially the highly colored variety, was found to be pure, and no violations were discovered.[98]

The confectionery business of the Greeks in the United States grew at a phenomenal rate throughout the country, especially between 1895 and 1915. By 1925, thousands of ice-cream parlors and candy shops were in existence in most of the large metropolitan areas of the country.[99] The following list, compiled in 1911, gives an indication of this:

City	Number of Confectioneries Owned by Greeks
Atlanta, GA	32
Baltimore	41
Birmingham, AL	15
Boston, MA	21
Buffalo, NY	11
Milwaukee, WI	17
Philadelphia, PA	19
San Francisco, CA	7
St. Louis, MO	19[100]

New York City also had a large number of shops since it was one of the main centers of the Greek population, but none of these could compare with Chicago. According to one estimate, there were approximately 925 confectionaries in the city as early as 1906.[101] The local newspaper

---

[98] Fairchild, Greek Immigration to the United States, p. 170.
[99] Constant, "Employment and Business of the Greeks in the U.S.," Athene, (Summer 1946), p. 40.
[100] Fairchild, Greek Immigration to the United States, p. 166.
[101] Saloutos, The Greeks in the United States, p. 263.

Hellinikos Astir labeled the city as the "Mecca of the Candy business," noting that "practically every busy corner in Chicago is occupied by a Greek candy store." It also asserted that 70 percent of the Greek candy merchants who were doing business in other cities once lived in Chicago and received their training there as well.[102]

One of the largest and most popular of the confectionery chains in the city was the De Mets Candy Stores. This Greek concern, which started its business by opening a small shop on the South Side, in a short time, emerged as one of the most successful chain candy stores in the metropolitan area. The success of this organization was primarily due to the intelligence and foresight of its owner, Mr. De Mets, who emerged as one of the leaders of the Chicago business community. The Greek newspaper Saloniki followed his progress closely and often reported the openings of his new stores. The following article was printed in December, 1924, to announce one such opening on one of the city's most impressive streets:

> Monday was the opening day of a new and magnificent candy store by the rapidly progressing Greek concern of De Mets. This new candy store is the sixth established by this company and is located at 330 South Michigan Avenue. It is the most luxurious and magnificent of all the stores and is remarkable for the excellence of its artistic decoration. The Greek company operates all its stores, which are located in the Loop, in a very efficient way and this accounts for their success.[103]

In addition to the opening of a vast number of sweet shops in the city the Greeks established themselves as the leaders in the candy manufacturing business and supplied stores owned by their compatriots throughout the southern and western states. As the number of candy stores in the various

---

[102] "Chicago--Mecca of the Candy Business," Greek Star, p. 2.
[103] "The De Met's Store on Michigan Avenue," Saloniki, 13 December 1924, p. 2.

cities increased in number, the demand for new factories to furnish supplies more than doubled. By the early 1920's the Greeks of Chicago established themselves as the leaders in all phases of the candy business. Hundreds of salesmen were hired by the manufacturing companies to supply the confectioners with the needs of the trade.[104]

Foremost among the candy manufacturers were the Gallanis Brothers. The popularity of their brand of chocolates grew so rapidly they soon abandoned their small candy store and built a large factory to meet the increasing demand. Their company, known as Temptation Chocolates, became the largest of its kind in the United States by 1921. The chocolates were made in their airy and immaculate plant by expert candy makers who not only used superior ingredients in their products but made a certain type of chocolate that did not melt in warm weather. This became especially important for marketing purposes.

Saloniki, which often promoted various types of Greek-owned businesses, encouraged confectioners to buy Temptation products:

> We recommend the brand to all Greek confectionery dealers not only because of the superiority of the chocolates, but because the concern is a Greek one. By handling it, the dealer, the concern and the community will be benefitted.[105]

Because of the quality of their products and the successful advertising of the company by Greek newspapers and Hellenic business guides, the progressive and enterprising Gallanis Brothers established themselves as one of the leaders of candy manufacturing and distribution in the United States. The following list of selected businesses and their locations illustrates not only the extent to which this firm established business

---

[104] "Chicago--Mecca of the Candy Business," Greek Star, p. 2.
[105] "Temptation Candy Company," Saloniki, 18 June 1921, p. 1.

relationships in all regions of the country but also largely with American and non-Greek concerns:

Name	Location
Northwestern Candy Company	Des Moines, Iowa
Otterbach Brothers	Louisville, Kentucky
Peoria Candy Company	Peoria, Illinois
Edward Phillips & Sons Co.	Eau Claire, Wisconsin
Julius C. Larsen	Menomine, Michigan
Wynn-Knox Candy Co.	Birmingham, Alabama
Shoemaker and Volkert	Buffalo, New York
Roberts Candy Company	Nashville, Tennessee
Goodman Cigar Store	Great Falls, Montana[106]

There were many other leading Greek-owned candy manufacturers based in Chicago which distributed their products in the city and throughout the country. Among these were the Meteor Candy Company on West Division Street and Meras-Kataras Candy Company on 39th Street on the South Side.[107]

Many of the confectioners encountered difficulties involving various aspects of their trade, including the establishment of credit with the business community, lack of unity, competition from fellow-Greeks and native Americans, and the inability to utilize intelligent business methods in their own shops. Most of these problems were due to their own lack of experience, ignorance of American business practices, and the refusal of many arrogant storeowners to change their ways. This was especially prevalent during the early years.

Americans were unfamiliar with the dependability of most of the confectioners because the Greeks never bothered to establish credit with companies which supplied them with fixtures and other necessities of the trade. Since they bought almost everything for cash, they had no credit

---

[106] "Temptation Chocolates," Saloniki, 17 May 1924, p. 5.
[107] Nickolson, p. 44.

rating with local bureaus. Thus, they were deemed as unreliable by many American companies.

With the realization that the borrowing of funds was necessary for the maintenance and expansion of their businesses, they finally sought to establish credit. But obstacles such as their own ignorance and a refusal to cooperate interfered. When asked to answer questions regarding the value of their businesses, they gave evasive answers or none at all. They were suspicious and distrustful in not wanting anyone, including their competitors, to know the details of their financial position.

Many of their financial problems, especially in the smaller shops, were the result of poor management. Clever salesmen would convince the Greeks to purchase the most expensive and elaborate equipment, such as marble soda fountains, which were unnecessary for their success and would ultimately place them in debt for many years. As a result, many of the fixtures they bought became outdated and unpopular long before they were paid for. Many realized their mistakes after they had already made the commitments.[108]

Many of the owners did not understand the practical methods of advertising and failed to use them to enhance their businesses. Segments of the Greek community, including the press, were bewildered and surprised when they discovered the various types of posters and display material found in the windows of some of the confectioneries. Many of the products advertised were not even sold in the stores. For example, large signs advertising Fan Fizz were found in stores which did not carry it. A huge Coca-Cola sign was discovered over the door of a candy shop that didn't even have a soda fountain. Posters advertising Mecca and Fatima cigarettes took up a considerable amount of space in the windows and on the inside of an ice-cream parlor which did not carry these brands or any other type of tobacco products. When they should have advertised exactly what they offered to the public, these stores were promoting the products sold by non-Greek businesses and, by doing so, ultimately hurt themselves.

---

[108] Saloutos, The Greeks in the United States, p. 263.

Saloniki criticized the negative advertising tactics of the confectioneries and offered advice on how they could improve the stature of their businesses:

> We ask that all advertising material be removed and forever banished from the display windows. The windowpanes should gleam with cleanliness instead of displays of Turkish cigarettes with half-nude figures on them. We suggest slogans or mottos, such as "Homemade Candies." Tell the world that your candies are not only delicious but are made in accordance with the requirements of the pure food laws.[109]

Most of the confectioners were influenced by the advice of their compatriots and improved their establishments.

Because of the lack of unity among the businessmen engaged in this trade, many Greeks were forced to compete against one another, especially when a confectioner opened a business next door or on the same block where another Greek was already established. The two proprietors would then become fierce business rivals and resorted to unwarranted and unethical practices, such as insulting one another and condemning the quality of each other's products in the presence of other Greek businessmen and customers.[110]

Problems such as these brought forth pleas from the Greek community for the confectioners to stop bickering among themselves and make a concerted effort to settle their differences. Once again, the newspapers were instrumental in offering suggestions to the businessmen. The Greek Press boldly recommended that it would be in the best interest of certain confectioneries which were located on the same street to merge with one another and form one large establishment. By doing so, they would eliminate competition between themselves, cut their costs in half, and ultimately, make more money.

---

[109] "The Confectioners," Saloniki, 3 June 1916, p. 2.
[110] Saloutos, The Greeks in the United States, p. 264.

They cited the case of four such establishments which they believed could benefit by their suggestion for unity. Their names were "Syros," "Phoenix," "Athenian," and "Smyrna." All were established, popular shops on South Halsted Street, and each earned a reputation for serving high quality products and maintaining a clean and organized establishment.

The total amount of yearly rental payments for the four stores amounted to $4,080; electricity and gas cost $1,365 annually; telephones cost approximately $240 a year; and miscellaneous items such as permits, licenses, and repairs amounted to $900 a year. The total of all the operating costs was $6,385 per year. The Greek Press argued that if all four establishments united into one large business, the yearly operating expense would probably amount to only $2,500. The combined firm would save $3,885 for the year and the additional sum could be used to increase the wages of the employees and provide the four partners with a substantial increase in their weekly income. Also, the daily purchasing costs would be substantially reduced and the expenditure of capital would decrease.

> Our respected confectioners must realize the truth of the above assertions. They must examine them with the sound economic part of their mind and not with the egoistic part. All the minor difficulties of such an arrangement could be easily smoothed out. We want an acceptance of the principle which has been used so successfully by American businessmen.[111]

The four owners agreed to discuss the proposition but failed to take the necessary steps toward unity.

Although many thought the proposal by the Greek Press was a logical one, there were other existing problems in the Greek business community which had to be resolved. Some of the shop-owners had difficulties within their own businesses and often had disputes with their partners. In such cases an individual usually underestimated the ability and value

---

[111] "Halsted Street Confectioners," Greek Press, 11 April 1935, p. 1.

of his associates and considered himself the most important figure in the business. When one person possessed this type of egoistic attitude, it obviously offended the others and would often culminate in resentment, quarreling, and mistrust. Many of the disputes among business partners were serious enough to warrant court litigation.

Saloniki argued that the reason for the failure of most of the partnerships was not egotism but the lack of business knowledge, proper training, and the failure of those involved to follow successful and systematic methods in the operation of their shops. In an article entitled, "Why Greek Partnerships Fail," they suggested that unless progressive and advanced methods were adopted, the impending failure of the partnerships was inevitable. They gave many suggestions and urged the Greeks to learn the details of how American-owned businesses operate:

> In American business organizations every one of the partners performs the duty to which he is assigned, just like a machine, without interfering with somebody else's duty and activity. Consequently, each recognizes the service of the other, and obediently takes and executes orders from his other partners who are wisely chosen to execute efficiently their respective responsibilities. The Americans succeed because they are equipped with business knowledge minus blind egotism.[112]

Another Greek-language newspaper not only advocated the adoption of American business methods but also encouraged its readers to adopt local customs and traditions.

> Let us Americanize ourselves. We make our bread and butter in America. We deal and trade with American people; we breathe free American air. Let us adopt the best they have, and let us unite ourselves with the best

---

[112] "Why Greek Partnerships Fail," Saloniki, 10 July 1926, p. 1.

friends that Greeks could ever wish for. America and Americanization are our best friends and protectors.[113]

The Greek businessmen, however, realized that many of the assertions, such as those mentioned above, were not necessarily correct. The xenophobic sentiment in the American community and the opposition to foreign-owned businesses which prevailed during the early years of the peddling and boot-blacking trades never really ceased to exist.

Proprietors never considered their businesses as being fully secure and were often suspicious that the local city government would initiate new legislation which could hurt them. The City of Chicago tried many times, for example, to pass an ordinance to prevent the candy stores from opening on Sundays. Since this was one of their busiest and most profitable days, the impact of this move would have been significant. Although the ordinance was never passed, the Greeks realized that without some form of unity, they were virtually helpless when threatened from the outside.

Efforts toward unity were partially fulfilled in 1919 with the formation of a Greek confectioner's association. It is difficult to assess the accomplishments of this group since no records of their meetings have been found, but, nevertheless, it was indicative of the willingness of the Greeks to unite and this, in itself, was considered an accomplishment.[114]

Six years later a group of candy-makers, known as Tzitziniotes, decided to combine their efforts, knowledge, and past experiences into an organization which, among other things, guaranteed them a saving of up to 24 percent in their buying. The group consisted of more than two hundred candy shop owners who hailed from the village of Tzitzinia in southern Greece. The Chicago Greek Daily applauded the formation of the group and hoped it would influence Greeks in other trades to do the same.[115]

Immediately following the First World War the greatest threat to the independently owned candy stores were the large American corporations

---

[113] Saloutos, The Greeks in the United States, p. 213.
[114] Ibid., p. 264.
[115] "Candymakers Form Organization," Chicago Greek Daily, 18 August 1925, p. 1.

which began establishing chains of department stores, candy shops, and drug stores throughout the country. The drug stores were especially precarious to the Greeks when they began installing confectionery counters and soda and ice cream fountains. They were considered by many as miniature department stores because they sold other items such as groceries, books, jewelry, tobacco, and hardware. Some even contained restaurants.[116]

The first chain drug stores originated in New York and Chicago, but by the mid 1920's, thousands of them appeared in both large cities and small towns. They not only accentuated competition with the Greek-owned stores, but were determined in becoming the dominant force in the business.[117] While formerly no other nationality could compete with the Greeks, the chain stores, with huge amounts of capital behind them, placed the individual candy-makers in an awkward position. Dr. Constantine Kalonzis, a spokesman and influential figure in the Greek community, believed that despite the bleak outlook of the current threat, the Greeks had sufficient capital, intelligence, and a capacity for organization to prevent themselves from being "devoured" by the corporate moguls.[118]

The <u>Greek Press</u>, which referred to the chains as "unjust monopolies," observed the situation differently. It stated that perhaps 15,000 of its co-nationals living in the United States would be directly affected by the emerging menace and even feared the eventual disappearance of the Greek businessman. The only means of survival, they argued, was through total unity and a modification of their businesses to include similar items being sold in the drug stores.[119]

Only the large and financially sound candy stores, however, were able to survive and compete with the corporate chains. Many of these were enlarged, radically remodeled, and offered new services to the public such as lunch counters or luncheonettes.

---

[116] "Greek Trade is in Peril," <u>Greek Press</u>, 3 July 1929, p. 1.
[117] Ibid., p. 2.
[118] "The Greek Merchants in Chicago," <u>Saloniki</u>, 25 January 1930, p. 3.
[119] "Greek Trade is in Peril," <u>Greek Press</u>, p. 2.

During the initial stages of depression, which included the early 1930's, most of the small confectioners who could not afford to modernize their stores and adopt new methods suffered from high overhead costs and were eventually driven out of business.[120]

A field which offered the Greek businessmen relative security, greater contact with the native American public, and a stable foundation upon which to amass a great amount of wealth was the restaurant business. The Greek restaurateurs, like their compatriots who entered the confectionery business, did not possess any special talent in the preparation and service of food, either in their homeland or in the United States. They learned the business mostly by working for others and by eventually opening establishments of their own. The restaurant business appealed to them because it did not require great skill or special training to be successful. Their aim was to learn the trade, understand what the public wanted, work very diligently to please them, and develop a profitable business which did not require exorbitant overhead costs.[121]

The first restaurants were those which served Greek cuisine. Many of the Greeks who patronized them not only helped their compatriots establish and maintain their businesses, but were influenced into opening small restaurants of their own. The first such Greek-cuisine restaurant in the United States, called the "Peloponnesos," was opened in 1857 on Roosevelt Street in New York City by Spyros Bazanos.[122] The majority of the Greeks during the first twenty years of the immigration, however, did not realize the potential this field offered, and it was not until approximately 1900 that any substantial number decided to become restaurant men. During the first decade of the twentieth century thousands of Greeks, especially in New York and Chicago, opened restaurants.[123]

---

[120] Constant, "Employment and Business of the Greeks in the U.S.," <u>Athene</u> (Summer, 1946), p. 41.
[121] Saloutos, <u>The Greeks in the United States</u>, p. 265.
[122] Theodore N. Constant, "Employment and Business of the Greeks in the U.S.," <u>Athene</u> VII (Autumn 1946), p. 28.
[123] Ibid., p. 29.

During the early years in Chicago most of the Greeks operated moveable lunch wagons and roamed the industrial districts of the city serving items such as hot dogs, sandwiches, and tamales to the factory workers. This service, which was the busiest everyday between 11 a.m. and 1 p.m., became very popular with the workers, and a high percentage of them discarded their lunch pails in favor of the more appetizing food offered by the Greeks.[124]

The traveling lunch counters were soon abandoned and replaced by established restaurants at permanent locations, primarily because of a city ordinance initiated by Mayor Carter Harrison II which outlawed the selling of food on the streets. Initially, the Greeks thought of protesting against the new ruling but no action was taken. They probably realized, instead, that by opening small restaurants in the same factory districts, they would probably make more money by offering an expanded variety of food to the workers at low prices.

Since most of them did not have the necessary capital to succeed, they formed partnerships with other Greeks, thus assuring themselves of meeting the initial expenses required. The saying that, "when two Greeks meet, they open up a restaurant," probably originated during this time.[125]

Some of the early restaurants were owned by families. These establishments were considered among the more successful because the workers, as a family group, were more willing to tolerate the long hard hours and various difficulties which arose. The family members, unlike employees hired from the outside, realized that they all shared in the ownership and were willing to sacrifice their time and effort for the welfare and future success of their business.[126]

Although the Greeks did not necessarily exceed their competitors in the preparation of food, they endeavored to purchase the highest quality possible from reputable and nationally advertised companies. A careful investigation of this matter was conducted by the Greek Star in 1919, and

---

[124] "The Greek as a Restaurant Man," Greek Star, 14 November 1919, p. 4.
[125] Saloutos, The Greeks in the United States, p. 266.
[126] Ibid., p. 267.

in only a few cases could their representatives find that inferior products were purchased by Greeks. It was learned that the vast majority bought their meat from standard concerns such as Swift, Armour, Morris, and Wilson. Canned goods were purchased from reputable wholesale grocers in Chicago and vegetables from leading firms at the South Water Market.

The only establishments found to be using second quality foodstuffs were those which were located in the poorer sections of the city where the patrons could not afford to pay for high grade food. One restaurateur interviewed by the Greek Star however, indicated that he had failed in business on two different occasions because he served high quality food in low-income neighborhoods. Since it was impossible for him to charge high prices, his refusal to buy low-grade products eventually resulted in the failure of his businesses.[127]

The greatest period of growth in the restaurant industry, as experienced by Greek immigrants, was during and after the First World War. Money was available, and the demand for food-service businesses coincided with an expanding national economy.[128] In 1919 it is said that one out of every three restaurants in Chicago was owned by a Greek. A high percentage of these were located in highly-populated areas, expanding neighborhoods, and in the downtown business district.[129] Although they were not known to have operated any cabarets which offered a combination of dining, dancing, and live entertainment, many Greeks saw the opportunity of opening restaurants in the night-club and entertainment districts of the city.[130] The average amount of money invested in a restaurant at this time was usually between three and five thousand dollars, with the total amount in Chicago exceeding $8,000,000. Their daily business averaged half a million dollars, and as a group in the United States it is said to have been ten times this amount.[131]

---

[127] "The Greek as a Restaurant Man," Greek Star, p. 10.
[128] Constant, "Employment and Business of the Greeks in the U.S.," Athene (Autumn 1946), p. 28.
[129] "The Greek as a Restaurant Man," Greek Star, p. 4.
[130] Saloutos, The Greeks in the United States, p. 268.
[131] "The Greek as a Restaurant Man," Greek Star, p. 4.

In 1921 Chicago became the leading city in the country in the number of Greek-owned food-service establishments totaling 560. The closest competitor was New York with 450. The number of similar restaurants in other cities and towns varied in proportion to their populations. In cities that were considered small in comparison to large urban centers such as Chicago, Boston, or Philadelphia, the number of Greek-owned restaurants were surprisingly numerous. In Flint, Michigan, for example, more than twenty restaurants were owned and operated by Greeks.[132]

By 1923 the number in Chicago soared to 1,035. Many aggressive owners who became extremely successful had the opportunity to expand their businesses throughout the city. It was not uncommon, therefore, for one Greek to own a chain of five, ten, or even twenty restaurants.[133] One of the leading figures in this type of endeavor was John Raklios, who arrived in 1900 without knowledge of the language and American business methods, yet was able to become one of the most successful restaurateurs in the history of the city. After the success of his first restaurant, which opened in 1906, he began opening other establishments in the downtown business district and throughout the city.[134]

By 1920 his efforts had become so lucrative that he decided to form a corporation together with two associates, Andrew Chrones and Vassili Kotsones. Through their united effort the Raklios Company, which owned and operated approximately thirty-five establishments by 1926, was not only foremost among Greek restaurant concerns but was competing with the largest American organizations for leadership in the business.[135]

All of the Greek newspapers contributed in announcing the openings of the restaurants and praising the Raklios Company for its outstanding

---

[132] Constant, "Employment and Business of the Greeks in the U.S.," <u>Athene</u> (Autumn 1946), p. 28.
[133] Ibid., p. 29.
[134] "John Raklios and Company Leases New Store on Randolph Street," <u>Saloniki</u>, 13 March 1926, p. 8.
[135] "A Half-Million Dollar Lease," <u>Chicago Greek Daily</u>, 19 July 1926, p. 1.

achievements throughout the years. The Chicago Greek Daily reported one such opening in April, 1926:

> Yesterday, on the corner of Jackson Boulevard and Halsted Street, a new restaurant of Raklios and Company was opened for business. This restaurant is a real jewel and gives to one of the most centrally located corners of Chicago a strong vitality. Herein lies the importance of the Raklios Restaurants, that they beautify the city of Chicago wherever they are located.[136]

Salonika reported the same opening and said, "The Greek chain store firm adds one more restaurant to its cloister. Raklios and Company stands out as a symbol of what could be done when two or more Greeks are united in any enterprise."[137] In yet another article written by Saloniki, it praised the remarkable guidance and leadership qualities of the administrators of the company: "These three compatriots of ours began their careers as poor immigrants and by hard work, honesty, and commercial ability. They are evidence of the splendid commercial spirit of the Greeks."[138]

John Raklios displayed an almost fearless attitude toward the consummation of his goals by taking many risks and spending an enormous amount of money. After he agreed to lease a store in the downtown Capitol building in 1926, he immediately spent more than $50,000 in equipping it as a high quality restaurant.[139] Three years earlier, his organization agreed to pay rentals amounting to approximately $500,000 in the leasing of an entire building on the corner of Madison and Clark Streets. This amount, which covered an undisclosed number of years, was the highest ever paid for an equal space on Madison Street. An additional $70,000 was then

---

[136] "New Restaurant Opened," Chicago Greek Daily, 30 April 1926.
[137] "The New Restaurant of Raklios and Company," Saloniki, 27 February 1926.
[138] "A New Commercial Success," Saloniki, 6 September 1924, p. 2.
[139] "John Raklios and Company Leases New Store on Randolph Street," Saloniki, p. 8.

spent on decorating it and making it one of the most attractive restaurants in the downtown district.[140]

All of the negotiations concerning the Raklios Company were handled by the real estate firm of George Tsiagouris, which was the oldest and most successful Greek-owned business of its kind in the city. Founded in 1908, the organization assisted many Greek businessmen in the rental of stores, the purchasing of property, and the furnishing of information concerning other real estate opportunities which existed in the Chicago area.[141] Because of his association with the largest realty firms in the city, Mr. Tsiagouris was able to conduct negotiations and finalize agreements on any building or enterprise. The Chicago Greek Daily praised the efforts of its compatriot:

> The business of Tsiagouris owes its success to the alertness and method with which he does his work and even more to his sincerity. The fact that Raklios and Company entrusts the leasing of space for its restaurants only to the offices of Mr. Tsiagouris, and that in a brief period $1,060,000 worth of leases were successfully negotiated for, demonstrates the character and ability of Mr. Tsiagouris. We really are not exaggerating when we say that his offices are the ablest in Chicago.[142]

While many restaurant-keepers were successful and able to please their customers and the community as a whole, others did not fare as well and were the objects of criticism by their patrons and the Greek and American press as well. A common complaint against many proprietors was that they failed to adhere to the basic standards of sanitation in maintaining their restaurants. Patrons who saw employees wearing stained and dirty uniforms or an owner who neglected to shave for several days became disillusioned and never returned. Equally as pitiful were chefs and

---

[140] "Successful Business," Saloniki, 17 February 1923, p. 5.
[141] "A New Commercial Success," Saloniki, p. 2.
[142] "A Half-Million Dollar Lease," Chicago Greek Daily, p. 1.

dishwashers with dirty hands and faces. Many of their washrooms were poorly ventilated, badly lighted, and were without clean towels or soap and contained faucets that were either broken or furnished only cold water.

Some employees made matters worse by leaving their dirty clothes hanging behind the door or piled on a chair next to the sink. Such conditions only served to alienate owners from the public. "In the light of his impressions from the washroom and the kitchen," argued the Greek Press, "you can easily understand why so many Greeks complain about the smallness of the American appetite. It is a wonder any customer ever has any appetite left."[143]

Many of the owners did not succumb to the harsh criticism and denied that their restaurants were unclean. Surprisingly, certain city officials agreed with them. In 1919, John Dill, the Commissioner of Health, wrote a letter which stated:

> The Department has no record of Greek restaurants segregated from the records operated by all nationalities, but the experience of the Department of Inspection is such that the claim could not be made that Greek restaurants were different in rank as regards sanitation and methods from other restaurants.[144]

Complaints concerning the quality of food in many restaurants were also voiced by a few citizens, although it was generally argued that most of the food served in Greek establishments was of high quality. In a precautionary effort directed toward the owners, however, Saloniki periodically reminded them of their duty to maintain high standards at all times. The Greeks, they argued, because they predominated in catering throughout the United States, were entrusted with a very important duty to perform and were responsible for the welfare of their customers. In an article entitled, "The

---

[143] "Advice to the Restaurants," Greek Press, 21 March 1935, p. 1.
[144] Saloutos, The Greeks in the United States, p. 268.

Restaurant Man," <u>Saloniki</u> discussed the importance of its message to the owners:

> The Greek must be proud of his trade and must devote his body and soul in performance of his duty. The preparation of food must be done by expert help, the selection and utilization of good quality victuals, cleanliness in the superlative, and politeness must be his responsibility. Thus his patrons will not only enjoy the good and nicely prepared food, but also will be satisfied psychologically. The delicate and important trade of the Greek restaurateur cannot be overestimated.[145]

The press tried to inform the restaurant-keepers that in addition to cleanliness and the serving of good food, the image of the proprietor was an important factor in business. The owner who projected arrogance, or perhaps laziness, by sitting around the store with a cigar in his mouth, or who hurried to collect a patron's money but moved slowly and somewhat indifferently when asked for a second cup of coffee was insulting his customers without realizing it.[146]

Another major criticism of the press was the apparent lack of an accounting system in many of the stores. The failure of a considerable number of establishments, they argued, was due to ignorance of the use of figures and a lack of any accounting experience. When asked about their bookkeeping methods, the response of the owners was usually the same: "I have a system; I know what I am doing." These owners knew how to add up profits but failed to deduct their losses and expenses. The <u>Chicago Greek Daily</u> sought to correct this by providing examples of proper bookkeeping in many of their articles.[147]

The restaurateurs, like the confectioners, realized that unity was necessary to defend themselves against criticism and hostility by their

---

[145] "The Restaurant Man," <u>Saloniki</u>, 17 December 1927, p. 1.
[146] Saloutos, <u>The Greeks in the United States,</u> p. 269.
[147] "The Greek Restaurant in America," <u>Chicago Greek Daily,</u> 12 July 1929, p. 1.

business adversaries and certain segments of the community. One of the first organizations to be formed in Chicago was the Greek Restaurant Keepers Association. This group, also known as the Hermes Association, did not achieve much cooperation primarily because of the rivalry which existed between two of its largest constituents, the Tripolitsiotas, who came from Tripolis, and the Spartans.[148]

More important was the formation of the American Association of Greek Restaurant Keepers in 1919. This group was able to succeed because it followed the same format used by successful American organizations. Qualified individuals were elected to govern the body and they determined by vote the amount to be paid for annual membership. They also agreed that anyone who was willing to work for the organization on a full-time basis should be paid a salary for his services. The association rented a large suite of offices in the downtown district to be used by members and their friends for business meetings and for social gatherings. Individual members could also use the office facilities for their own personal business transactions.[149]

Foremost among the objectives of the organization was to raise the standards of customer service, food, sanitation, working environment, and to assist owners in meeting health regulations. It urged its members to adopt American ideals and business practices and to become citizens of the United States. A high priority of the group was to resist prejudicial and untruthful statements on the part of the community directed toward the business practices of the Greeks.[150]

Mandatory prerequisites in the attainment of their objectives were to establish better relations with the public and by cooperating with prominent Americans in the city, such as bankers, lawyers, merchants, and other professional people. They wanted to display their respect and admiration toward their newly-adopted country in order to prove that Greeks were an asset to the communities in which they lived and worked.[151]

---

[148] Saloutos, The Greeks in the United States, p. 267.
[149] "American Association of Greek Restaurant-Keepers," Saloniki, 2 August 1924, p. 1.
[150] Saloutos, The Greeks in the United States, p. 268.
[151] "American Association of Greek Restaurant-Keepers," Saloniki, p. 1.

The restaurant owners also felt the threat of increased competition during the 1920's, including that of the chain store, but most of the failures were due to poor management and unprogressive business practices rather than harassment from the American community.[152]

Another field which became both popular and successful for the Greeks was the fruit business. Although the number of fruit stores did not come close to equaling the number of restaurants or confectioneries, the Greeks nevertheless displayed their initiative by eventually dominating the business in both Chicago and New York. At first, fruits were mostly sold in candy shops or grocery stores as an added attraction to the main stock, but as the demand began to increase, separate businesses were opened.

In contrast to the candy shops, which began to decline after the First World War amid competition from the American corporations, the fruit stores experienced their greatest period of growth as thousands of them opened throughout the country. In 1921 the Greeks of Chicago owned ninety retail fruit stores, twenty-six fruit and vegetable stores, and eight fruit wholesale businesses. If the number of small fruit stands were added, the total number was even greater. Four years later the number of retail fruit stores rose to 385 with wholesalers totaling 18. Many successful fruit dealers owned more than one store.

As the field expanded, owners enlarged their stores and offered a wide range of products to their customers such as canned goods, meats, liquor, and dairy products. Thus, the fruit store became a general market store.[153]

Unlike their compatriots in other fields, the fruit dealers did not experience the difficulties which evolved from petty rivalries and the lack of unification. Although the reason for this is unknown, efforts toward cooperation and unity were displayed by the fruit dealers as early as 1916 when they formed the Greek Fruit Company. Their primary objective, according to president John Vasilopoulos, was to pool their resources and buy greater quantities of fruit at lower prices.[154]

---

[152] Saloutos, The Greeks in the United States, p. 270.
[153] Constant, "Employment and Business of the Greeks in the U.S.," Athene (Summer 1946), p. 41.
[154] "Unification," Saloniki, 15 April 1916.

One of the cleanest and most pleasant enterprises the immigrants engaged in was the floral business. Their love for flowers was traditional and considered an indispensible part of Greek life. In ancient Greece wreaths, garlands, and flowers were highly symbolic when used in rites, celebrations, marriages, funerals, and the Olympic games.[155]

Those who opened flower shops in Chicago found the business to be very profitable, easy to operate, and without strong competition from other nationalities. They considered it pleasant to work in an atmosphere filled with aromatic flowers and selling them to a better class of patrons.[156]

Peter Andreou worked in a flower shop owned by his father in the railroad station in Columbus, Ohio, before the family decided to move to Chicago. He discussed the various aspects of the business as he remembered them:

> The Union Station people didn't want a peanut stand because it would get too dirty. Flowers were acceptable and they were the ones who actually gave my father the idea. We bought them from Greek-owned greenhouses in Chicago and they would send them to us by train. I would pick them up at the station and the only thing we had to do was trim them and put them in water.[157]

He maintained there was no business during the summer months because flowers were in abundance and people could go out and pick their own. In spite of this, his father made approximately $500 during the remainder of the year and considered it very profitable.[158]

Although there were only thirteen Greek-owned flower shops in Chicago in 1923, as compared with 175 in New York, this number did not include the numerous small flower stands throughout the former

---

[155] "The Flowers Sellers," Saloniki, 6 August 1927.
[156] Constant, "Employment and Business of the Greeks in the U.S.," Athene (Summer 1946), p. 41.
[157] Interview with Peter Andreou, Berwyn, Illinois, 18 March 1982.
[158] Ibid.

city. Also, many expanded their businesses to include flower gardens and greenhouses. These individuals became the wealthiest in the floral industry.[159]

Before the outbreak of the First World War the American people became increasingly interested in new and expanding forms of entertainment which were available to them. Chicago became one of the leading cities in the country in the construction of theatres, ballrooms, and motion-picture houses with Greek businessmen playing a significant role in their development.[160]

Because the motion picture was the newest and most popular form of entertainment during this time, a number of Greeks entered the business and were extremely successful in the operation of both small and large neighborhood movie theatres. Many of these were people who had been established in other businesses, such as restaurants or confectioneries, and recognizing the potential of the film industry, decided to open movie houses close to their stores. A second-generation Greek woman recalled her father's continuous search for profitable investments:

> In 1910 my father owned a candy store in the Bohemian neighborhood of 22nd Street and Kedzie Avenue. He decided to open a movie theatre next door because he believed he could make money and the people in the neighborhood would enjoy it. He owned the property because he bought it a few years before. He had to go to Balaban & Katz everyday to pick up the movies. The theatre did very well.[161]

She added that the reason he was able to open a new business was because he saved a huge sum of money by renting an apartment to live in, rather

---

[159] Constant, "Employment and Business of the Greeks in the U.S.," Athene (Summer 1946), p. 41.
[160] Theodore N. Constant, "Employment and Business of the Greeks in the U.S.," Athene VII (Winter 1947), p. 38.
[161] Interview with Mary Moraitis, Forest Park, Illinois 5 October 1981.

than buying a home. The money was used for investment purposes rather than the pleasures of living. She maintained this was the procedure followed by successful Greek businessmen.

By the early 1920's Greeks who concentrated in the movie business were able to open chains of theatres throughout the city. Individuals who were among the most successful in accomplishing this were Vassilli Vasilopoulos, Triphon Valos, James Coston, John Manta and Van Nomikos.[162]

One of the largest circuits in Chicago was operated by the Gregory Brothers, who also built theatres in Indiana, northern Illinois, Iowa, and the west coast.[163] In addition to financing and operating their establishments, the brothers contributed their own ideas in both their construction and design. Movie houses owned by them were considered among the most beautiful and modern in the city by the public and the press. In 1924 Saloniki announced the grand opening of a Gregory Company theatre in suburban Berwyn. They described the new Parthenon Theatre as 'luxurious,' and noted the cost of constructing such a high-quality building was in excess of $600,000. The company also built movie theatres for other Greeks who were interested in the business.[164]

The leading and perhaps most famous entrepreneur in Chicago's entertainment industry was Andrew Karzas. The Greek immigrant was responsible for the construction of the largest and most artistically designed theatres and ballrooms in the city, and perhaps the country. Two of his movie theatres, the North Center on the North Side near Lincoln Avenue and Robey Street, and the other in Hammond, Indiana were built in 1925 at an estimated total cost of $3,300,000.[165] One year later, he surpassed himself by announcing plans for the construction of the New Woodlawn Theatre on the South Side at an estimated cost of $5,000,000. The theatre, which would take more than a year to complete, would almost cover an entire square block area bounded by 63rd Street, Maryland Avenue,

---

[162] Constant, "Employment and Business of the Greeks in the U.S.," Athene (Winter, 1947), p. 38.
[163] "Grand Opening of a New Theatre," Saloniki, 20 September 1924, p. 1.
[164] "Form Greek Enterprise," Saloniki, 2 February 1924, p. 1.
[165] "Greek Progress in Business," Saloniki, 16 May 1925, p. 4.

Drexel Boulevard, and 63rd Place. Its interior decoration was to be of Persian design, and the stage area was to be an exact replica of New York's Metropolitan Opera House. He hoped it would earn the reputation of being the largest and most beautiful movie palace in the world.[166]

In 1922, Mr. Karzas and his partners spent over $1,000,000 to build the Trianon Ballroom, considered one of the most magnificent dancing halls in the world.[167] After the building was remodeled in 1935, it was visited by the editor of the Greek Press, who discussed his impressions of both the original building and the way it appeared after improvements were made:

> Despite the fact that many visits to the Trianon have impressed me to the beauty of the foyer and the curving staircase, nevertheless, I could not help but recall the first time I visited this world-famous ballroom. That was in 1922. I could not believe my eyes, for never had I or anyone else seen anything to compare with it. However, when I saw it this last time, it was as if it were a new creation made by a magic wand. Everything is new-- from the ceilings to the floors. Tapestries, paintings, and draperies, chair and divan covers, color combinations and effects--all have been changed. The effect is marvelous.[168]

Three years after the Trianon was built, Mr. Karzas furnished the citizens of Chicago with yet another dancing hall which would exceed any other in both decoration and cost. The new ballroom, called the Aragon, was constructed on the corner of Lawrence and Winthrop Avenues on the North Side at a cost of $2,000,000.[169]

Despite the enormous success of Chicago's Greeks in the entertainment field they were, nevertheless, surpassed by compatriots who operated in

---

[166] "Andrew Karzas Builds a $5,000,000 Theatre," Saloniki, 21 August 1926, p. 6.
[167] "Andrew Karzas," Saloniki, 8 December 1922.
[168] "Trianon is Redecorated," Greek Press, 10 October 1935, p. 1.
[169] "Greek Progress in Business," Saloniki, p. 4.

different regions of the country, primarily on the west coast.[170] One of them was Alexander Pantages, who emigrated from Andros, Greece as a young boy, became a circus hand in California, and emerged as the owner of one of the largest theatrical chains on the west coast. Mr. Pantages, known as the "King of Theatres," managed his business from Seattle, Washington.[171]

The largest and most famous Greek-owned theatre chain in the world was owned by the Skouras Brothers: Charles, George, and Spyros. Their first goal as young immigrant boys was to buy a nickelodeon, and they accomplished this by working at a series of odd jobs in restaurants and hotels. By 1926 they owned and operated thirty-seven movie theaters in St. Louis, Missouri. By 1945, they became leaders in the international film industry when their operation included 750 theatres throughout the United States, with 450 more in foreign countries, such as Australia, New Zealand, England, and Egypt.[172] The brothers received additional influence and prestige when one of them, Spyros, became president of Twentieth Century-Fox Film Corporation in 1942.[173]

Other types of businesses which may be considered as part of the entertainment field were billiard rooms, pool halls, and bowling alleys. Often, any one of these was operated in conjunction with other businesses such as restaurants, hot-dog stands, or shoe-shine parlors.[174] One immigrant who, at one time or another, was involved in all three concerns discussed his progression from being a pool player to the owner of several businesses:

> I used to hang around pool rooms playing pool for money. One of these was owned by a Greek. I was a good pool player and the guy liked me. He suggested that I operate a

---

[170] Constant, "Employment and Business of the Greeks in the U.S.," Athene (Winter 1947), p. 38.
[171] Xenides, p. 83.
[172] Louis Adamic, A Nation of Nations (New York: Harper Brothers Publishers, 1944), p. 277.
[173] Constant, "Employment and Business of the Greeks in the U.S.," Athene (Winter 1947), p. 38.
[174] Constant, "Employment and Business of the Greeks in the U.S.," Athene (Autumn 1946), p. 29.

hamburger and hot-dog stand in the corner so the players could get something to eat. I could also hustle pool at the same time. Before long I opened up a pool hall of my own at 47th and Ashland. It was a good business. Later, I had my eye on the bowling alley nearby. I was able to buy it from Brunswick with no money down because they knew about me from my pool hall. They thought I would be a good risk. I always wanted to be in business by myself.[175]

One of the largest entertainment centers in the city was built in 1924 by the Rhegas Brothers and Panagiotes Domigeles. Their establishment, known as the Pioneer Arcade, contained billiard and pool tables, twenty bowling lanes, and other various recreational activities. Built at a cost of more than $350,000 it was considered unique among establishments of its kind in the city.[176]

By 1923 there were more than one-hundred Greek-owned billiard and pool halls in the city. This industry, as it concerned Greeks and other ethnic groups, began to decline during the late 1920's when many of the owners established themselves in more permanent and respectable fields.[177]

The hotel business appealed to many Greek businessmen. Those who attained a certain degree of prominence in this field gained valuable experience by working as bus boys, dishwashers, head waiters, bell captains, and ultimately, as managers. After years of participating in the business, they opened small hotels of their own. Those who had been fortunate enough to work in elegant hotels in Athens, Salonica, Constantinople, and cities of the Near East learned much of the business long before they arrived in Chicago. Their high earnings and the elegant surroundings

---

[175] Interview with Stoes.
[176] "Progress Among Greeks," Saloniki, 5 July 1924, p. 3.
[177] Constant, "Employment and Business of the Greeks in the U.S.," Athene (Autumn 1946), p. 29.

certainly induced many of them to stay in the business.[178] By 1923, there were fifteen Greek-owned hotels in the city.[179]

Although the majority of the Greeks were proprietors of standard businesses such as shoe-shine parlors, restaurants, and confectioneries, the total number of fields involving Greek immigrants in Chicago in 1923 numbered approximately sixty and included 3,196 places of business. The following list is an example of some of these:

bakeries 11	coffee houses 25
banks 1	dancing schools 3
barber shops 39	dry goods stores 8
book stores 4	drug stores 2
candle manufacturers 2	employment offices 3
china & glassware 2	furriers 2
cigarette & cigar makers 6	hay & seed stores 4
coffee dealers 5	insurance agencies 23
jewelry stores 4	plumbing shops 2
laundries 3	printing shops 6
wholesale meat markets 3	range shops 3
music stores 3	real estate offices 29
publications 5	shoe-repair shops 85
phonograph stores 4	steamship agencies 6
photography studios 4	fixture stores 2
undertakers 2	tailor shops 8
pie & pastry shops 5	wholesale tobacco .... 1[180]

In an effort to assist their compatriots who were conducting business in Chicago, educated Greeks published a number of guides and directories which were used for advertising and listing places of business according

---

[178] Constant, "Employment and Business of the Greeks in the U.S.," Athene (Winter 1945), p. 39.
[179] Constant, "Employment and Business of the Greeks in the U.S.," Athene (Winter 1947), p. 40.
[180] Ibid.

to category. One of the most popular was the <u>Greek Directory of Chicago and Vicinity</u>, published in 1921 by the Nickolson Brothers. It was considered one of the most complete and informative in the city.[181] Aside from its importance to local businessmen, the directory proved useful to individuals who came from outside the area, or the country, and were eager to transact business with the local Greeks. American concerns which had established relationships with Greeks also found it advantageous to advertise in the guide. It provided important information concerning mortgages, contracts, bankruptcy laws, and explanations of other legal matters which businessmen found useful to know.[182]

The editor of the directory, George Nickolson, considered the publication as a milestone in the history of the Hellenic community:

> It is indeed true that many small guides have been published in the United States from coast to coast, but for a big community such as the Greek colony of Chicago, a perfect business guide should have been in existence long ago. The publishing of this book is meant to fill the gap which existed for a long time here. This is one of the mandatory supplements for the Greeks because they live in one of the most industrial cities in the world. The gap is now being filled.[183]

Advertisements were written in both Greek and English.

---

[181] Nickolson, p. 3.
[182] Ibid., p. 67.
[183] Ibid., p. 3.

CHAPTER V

PREJUDICIAL SENTIMENT DISPLAYED TOWARD THE GREEK BUSINESSMEN AND THEIR COMMUNITY

Go confidently in the direction of your dreams! Live the life you've imagined.

Henry David Thoreau

A continuing difficulty which confronted Greek businessmen, regardless of their particular trade, was the prejudicial sentiment on the part of the American community. Their presence in Chicago was resented by many, merely because they were foreigners. Much of the blame lies with the immigrants themselves. Whenever the community read about illegal activities in Greek coffeehouses, fraudulent Greek bankers, or restaurant owners who tried to take advantage of young female employees, it affected their image of the Greeks as a total ethnic group.

In 1909, Agamemnon Panagakis published a small newspaper of his own in which he advertised himself as a prominent investor and a great patriot, among other things. He offered many services to the Greek workers in Chicago, including an easy and rapid way to send money to their relatives and friends in Greece. Hundreds of hard-working laborers sought to take advantage of his services and entrusted him with their savings, only to discover that he fled the city several days later, taking all the money with him. Although it was rumored that he was in New York or Europe, his whereabouts remained unknown, and the investors never recovered their money. The news of this incident spread throughout the city and caused obvious embarrassment to the Greek community.[184]

Another unfortunate incident which received city-wide news coverage and involved Greek businessmen was the scandal concerning the Greek-American Bank in the summer of 1915. The four owners: George Douros, Fotios Papakostas, Angelos Geokaris, and George Stamatides, filed for

---

[184] "How the Greeks Must Send Their Money to Greece," Greek Star, 3 December 1909, p. 1.

bankruptcy and closed their businesses under the pretext that it was "due to the war in Europe." Some of the Greek newspapers supported the bankers and assured the 800 depositors, most of whom were ignorant and uninformed laborers, that they would receive their money in a short time. The press claimed that the bankers owned plantations in Greece and mines in Canada and that it would not be difficult to return the money, which amounted to approximately $215,000 dollars.[185]

The four bankers, who were brought to trial on embezzling charges, were found innocent and the depositors, who were unable to raise money for their defense, were viewed as being ignorant and indifferent by the Greek community. The management of Saloniki did not agree with the verdict.[186] They accused the four bankers of embezzlement and condemned the other newspapers for supporting their fraudulent activities. They published numerous articles in an effort to prove their position, appealing to the Greek community for support. One month later a committee was formed to investigate the matter and was successful in raising money to hire a defense attorney to represent the depositors. Their efforts to procure a new trial continued for many months without success. The bankruptcy caused a great commotion in Chicago.[187]

In 1907 a Greek confectioner by the name of Theodore Economakes was found guilty of forcing his attentions upon one of his young female employees and was sent to prison for a number of years. During the termination of the trial, Judge Frank Crowe aroused the anger of the entire Greek community when he stated, among his final remarks, that "all you Greek confectioners lead our girls astray." Influential members of the Greek community condemned the statement as false and unfair, and questioned the judge's professionalism in making such a remark. The Greek Star protested "that the spirit of Americanism is grossly violated and offended by unjust accusations against all Greeks.[188]

---

[185] "The Tragic History of the Greek-American Bank," Saloniki, 2 October 1915, p. 2.
[186] "The Guilty are Absolved," Saloniki, 9 October 1915.
[187] "Better Late Than Never," Saloniki, 23 October 1915.
[188] "The Crusade," Greek Star, 1 March 1907, p. 3.

The anger of the community was inflamed to such a degree that a mass meeting attended by more than 1800 confectioners was held to decide a proper course of action to deal with the matter. Also present were the publisher and editor of the Greek Star, prominent members of the American community, and representatives of the city press. The Greek leaders sought a retraction of the judge's statement and absolving Greek businessmen, in general, from any wrongdoing. Several days later, the judge apologized for his remarks and various American newspapers vindicated the Greek community in its stance against prejudice and unfairness. The editor of the Greek Star applauded the outcome but hoped the entire incident would serve as a warning to the businessmen.

> In order to avoid a repetition of this incident, the Star urgently appeals to all Greek confectioners, restaurant-keepers, and other who employ young women to bear in mind that if anyone is known to be indecently inclined, he should immediately be reported to the authorities. We shall not only protect society but also our own good name.[189]

One of the causes of prejudicial sentiment against Greek businessmen was the result of long-standing feuds which existed among store owners or between partners. Many who could not get along with one another engaged in arguments during business hours and in full view of those who were patronizing the store. The cause of these sudden outbursts was usually the result of misunderstandings concerning ownership status or the methods used in the operation of a business. Some of the altercations resulted in threats, physical fights, and even murder.

One of the better-known disputes in the Greek business community existed between the two owners of the flourishing Rousetos and Floros Ice Cream Company, namely Pantelis Rousetos and James Floros. Both of these successful businessmen desired complete control of the company and

---

[189] Ibid., p. 4.

each offered to buy the other's interest. Since neither was willing to leave, they continuously argued the matter and neglected to concern themselves with the daily obligations of the business. After one such heated argument in August, 1913, Mr. Rousetos shot and killed his partner with a small pistol.[190]

A similar incident occurred when Haralambos Bratsolias murdered his former grocery-store partner, George Bougioukos, after he was convinced that he had been defrauded of a large sum of money. Bratsolias then turned the gun on himself and committed suicide.[191] Although it was known that the Greeks possessed one of the lowest crime rates among ethnic groups in the city, incidents such as the murders of Floros and Bougioukos helped to foster a negative image on the group as a whole.[192]

A business which received much criticism from all segments of the community was the kaffeneion, or coffee-house. Men would congregate in these colorful places during various times of the day to read Greek newspapers, drink coffee, listen to music from home, and argue politics. Most of the subjects they discussed centered on current events in Greece: the Turks, the Balkan Wars, the patriotic leader Venizelos, and the political future of Greece. Others glorified themselves by repeating stories of Leonidas at Thermopylae and the conquests of Alexander the Great.

Another subject which undoubtedly received much attention was the *Megale Idhea*, or Great Idea. This concept, shared by many Greeks throughout the world, was the hope that Greece would someday be as large and culturally significant as the old Byzantine Empire which flourished in Constantinople for more than one-thousand years.[193]

The coffee-houses almost always had names significant in Greek culture and history. Some of the common ones were "Arcadia," "Parthenon," "Venizelos," "Macedonia," and "Acropolis." Many non-Greeks criticized

---

[190] "A Bloody Drama," Saloniki, 9 August 1913.
[191] "Murder and Suicide," Saloniki, 26 April 1930, p. 1.
[192] Ibid., p. 2.
[193] Thalia Cheronis Selz, "The Switchboard," Chicago, October 1976, p. 129.

its customers and suggested that men who frequented these places were lazy and tried to avoid working.[194]

Chicago mayor Carter Harrison criticized them as centers of vice and immorality when it became known that many of them served as centers for gambling. Police raids became periodic and many owners were fined. Mayor Harrison, with the support of many citizens, even suggested imposing a heavy tax on them.[195]

The newspapers gave considerable coverage to the raids, and the Greek community was obviously embarrassed. Many argued that the coffee-houses be closed. Others maintained that those not taking part in gambling be allowed to remain open. Many Greeks defended them as social centers that assisted recent immigrants in adjusting to their new environment. They maintained the gambling consisted only of card-playing and criticized the community's over-reaction to it. They stressed the benefits of the coffee-houses and pleaded they be allowed to exist.[196]

Despite the embarrassment suffered by the Greek community there was a humorous side to the newspaper coverage of the raids. Various headlines stated: "The Parthenon is Raided," "The Acropolis Closed," "Acropolis and Venizelos Taken," and "Parthenon and Seventeen Greeks Arrested." Some thought the humor of many of these statements alleviated some of the disgrace.

Greek community leaders urged the owners to operate clean and respectable shops and avoid any misconduct that would further demean the Greek image. Young men were encouraged to participate in other activities and avoid the coffee-houses as much as possible. Enrollment in evening classes and athletic activities were emphasized as alternatives. Eventually, with an increase in job opportunities and a more active family life, much interest in the coffee-house began to fade.[197]

Card-playing and lackadaisical behavior was not confined to the coffee-houses and was visible in other Greek-owned establishments. A

---

[194] Saloutos, The Greeks in the United States, p. 78.
[195] Ibid., p. 81.
[196] Ibid., p. 82.
[197] Selz, p. 131.

columnist for the Greek newspaper <u>Loxias</u> described several demeaning characteristics he witnessed while visiting businesses owned by compatriots.

> I entered a Greek confectionery one day and found six of my countrymen, seated around a table, playing <u>Skambili</u> (a Greek card game). Imagine what business the proprietor must be doing! What would the customers think upon entering a store and finding card-players taking up all the room? A thousand-dollar soda fountain and expensive fixtures--all sacrificed to card-players.[198]

Another time he saw several Greeks standing outside their store loudly criticizing a woman who passed by. They commented on the way she walked, the color of her hair, the way she dressed, and her physical attributes. "After such humiliation," he asked, "is it any wonder the woman does not patronize this store?"[199]

Greek businessmen were often bothered by customers and neighborhood hooligans and were the victims of physical abuse. Those who owned or worked in small shops and stores were harassed more frequently than others due to their visibility in the neighborhood. Dimitri Bartsakis, who worked as a waiter in a Greek-owned restaurant for eleven years, was constantly bothered by patrons.

He remembered a man who came in one day, sat in a booth, and ordered a hamburger. While waiting only a few minutes he grabbed a bottle of catsup, threw it against the wall, and walked out. Other individuals would pour their coffee into the sugar bowls while others were always attempting to start fights. Many customers walked out without paying for their food.

There were many Irish, Polish, and Czech club members in the neighborhood who frequented the restaurant periodically, causing more trouble than those who were alone. When they overheard the employees speaking Greek, they would call them names and ridicule them for

---

[198] "Progress and System," <u>Loxias</u>, 20 May 1909, p. 2.
[199] Ibid., p. 3.

speaking a different language. They were extremely aggressive and always demanded quick service. One of them, who protested the service was not satisfactory, actually broke the marble counter-top in two with a bottle. Mr. Bartsakis indicated that the owner called the police many times when such abuses occurred, but nothing was ever done. He labeled the troublemakers as "ignorant and low-class people," but maintained there was very little they could do.[200]

A second generation Greek recalled his father experiencing similar difficulties while operating a soda-fountain shop in a non-Greek area of the city. One particular incident was foremost in his recollections:

> One evening a mob gathered near my father's store and were waiting for him to close. They wanted to beat him up because he was an immigrant. A policeman came in and pretended to be friendly, and my dad obviously felt secure in having him around. He treated him to whatever he wanted and left with him so he could be protected. After he locked up and took a few steps the cop pulled a disappearing act. When he saw the mob close in on him he crashed through the line like a football player and ran for a mile. Sometime later he met one of them again and beat him severely. They never bothered him again.[201]

George Spelson (Spirotopoulos) and his brother opened a soda-fountain shop in suburban Forest Park with the financial assistance of an uncle. He recalled many instances of misconduct by local residents, and focused upon one man who walked in one summer day and almost immediately began shouting obscenities at the employees: "We are Americans and you are only foreigners. You are nothing but god-damn Greeks. Get the hell out of our country."[202] He added that this type of incident was not unique and took place periodically.

---

[200] Interview with Dimitri Bartsakis, Oak Park, Illinois, 23 September 1980.
[201] Interview with Nicholas Ellis, Chicago, Illinois, 1 October 1980.
[202] Interview with Spelson.

He admitted that verbal attacks were not confined to his store because he experienced them almost everywhere he went. On one occasion he was sitting on a train conversing in Greek with a friend when a man behind them overheard their conversation and ridiculed them for not speaking English. Mr. Spelson indicated to him that he need not listen and suggested placing cotton in his ears to avoid further annoyance. The stranger persisted in his demand that they cease speaking in a foreign language but soon found himself laid out on the floor after a punch by Mr. Spelson. He then got up, walked to the door, and got off at the next station without saying a word.[203]

This display of harassment and resentment is an indication that prejudicial sentiment on the part of Americans was not confined to the businessmen, but was directed toward the Greeks as an ethnic and foreign group. One immigrant who recalled experiences of prejudice was Thomas Spear (Spiropoulos), who came to the United States in 1911 from Corinth at age seventeen. He went directly to South Dakota to work for his uncle, a railroad foreman, and since most of the workers there were fellow-Corinthians, he believed this would be the appropriate place to begin a new life in America. He soon grew tired of the environment and decided to go to Chicago. After a series of odd jobs, he was hired as a waiter at the Palmer House, one of the city's most exclusive hotels. Here he encountered his first experiences of friction with non-Greeks.

After he established a fine work record, the manager decided to promote him to the position of head waiter. Since all the other men at this level were German, they resented a non-German being given the position and expressed their dissatisfaction immediately. The management refused to listen to complaints and maintained that Mr. Spear's promotion was based on his diligent record and not his national background. Being dissatisfied with the management's position, they began to harass their new co-worker on a daily basis. At first, Mr. Spear had no intention of complaining for fear of losing his job, but being unable to withstand the constant intimidation, he informed the manager as to what was occurring.

---

[203] Ibid.

The owner informed them that if they continued their behavior they would be dismissed from the hotel, so they ceased their attacks and everything seemingly returned to normal.[204]

Often, local newspapers accused the Greeks of committing crimes which they were neither guilty of nor involved in. In October, 1904, the <u>American</u>, a Chicago daily newspaper, reported that two Greeks named Fero and Milano were arrested for the murder of Santo Napolitano, a recent Italian immigrant who married a woman that Fero was said to have loved in Genoa, Italy, before emigrating to the United States. Upon learning that Napolitano and his bride were living in Chicago, Fero, with the assistance of his friend, Milano, broke into his home and murdered him.

Knowing that the names of the assassins were not Greek, the <u>Greek Star</u> investigated the matter and informed the <u>American</u>, and the other newspapers which printed the story, of the mistake. None of them bothered to correct the error in subsequent articles concerning the case.[205]

Harassment toward Greeks was evident in the less-populated cities and towns of Illinois as well as in Chicago. People in the smaller communities were not accustomed to large groups of foreigners and the Greeks became targets of ridicule, perhaps more so than their counterparts in the big city. Many Greek families tried to settle in the smaller towns before deciding to move to Chicago. Peter Voltes, a son of immigrant parents, reminisced about his childhood in Quincy, Illinois:

> When I was growing up there was a lot of prejudice against us because we were Greek. I remember they used to call us 'greaseballs.' They never left us alone. I studied very hard in school and became the top student only because there was nothing else for me to do. The other kids would never play with me because I was a foreigner. I had a lot of pride and the only way to prove myself was to become a good student.[206]

---

[204] Interview with Thomas Spear (Spiropoulos), Berwyn, Illinois, 17 September 1980.
[205] "The <u>American</u> is Misinformed," <u>Greek Star</u>, 7 October 1904, p. 3.
[206] Interview with Peter Voltes, Oak Park, Illinois, 26 September 1980.

Peter Valos, an immigrant whose parents settled in a smaller city before moving to Chicago's Greek Town, admitted to difficulties in adjustment:

> We came to the United States from Filiatra in 1923 and went directly to East Moline, Illinois. When I was a kid going to school the American students made fun of us all the time because we were Greek. They never let us alone. It was miserable! The Greek children had to stick together for companionship and protection. There was nothing else for us to do. They would make fun of me when I spoke Greek and tried to mimic my words all the time. I guess my parents felt this too because they never had any American friends. They were all Greek. All the Greeks stayed together.[207]

Resentment toward the Greeks was further aggravated during the outbreak of the Balkan Wars in 1912. Thousands of immigrants living in the United States returned to their homeland to assist in the struggle against the Turks. It is estimated that between 40,000 and 50,000 volunteers left United States ports, most of whom experienced fighting during 1912 and 1913. Many who could not go sent money. According to Thomas Burgess, author of Greeks in America:

> Splendid enthusiasm was displayed in every colony of Greeks in the United States.... That autumn and winter at our Atlantic seaports the crowds of embarking patriots were familiar and inspiring sights as they marched to the ships, singing their national anthem and receiving the final blessing from their priests.[208]

A considerable number of Chicago's Greeks took part in the struggle. There were many patriots who journeyed to all parts of the city in search

---

[207] Interview with Peter Valos, Forest Park, Illinois, 19 September 1980.
[208] Burgess, p. 85.

of volunteers. Their purpose was to appeal to their patriotism and inspire them to join in the conflict against their traditional enemy, the Turks. One immigrant vividly remembered the atmosphere created during that period:

> In 1912 George Petropoulos, a great patriot, went around to all the Greek coffee-houses, churches, and places of business in the city to tell them that Greece needed their help. He gathered 150 Greeks in the Halsted Street area alone. The Greek government paid their way. Only a few of them came back because most were killed and some stayed in Greece after the war.[209]

Patriotic sentiment toward the homeland by Chicago's Greeks was not limited to times of war. A woman who is a librarian, teacher, and daughter of an immigrant indicated that her father, who was also a volunteer during the Balkan struggle, was always thinking of ways to assist Greece in any way he could:

> My father never forgot the village where he came from in Greece. It's called Vouno, and it is near Tripolis. He knew the village needed a pipe system that would bring water down from the nearby mountain to irrigate the land properly, and he was determined to raise money for the project from his fellow-villagers living in the United States. He had all their names and addresses and went to see every one of them by train. He was working for the railroad at the time and had a free pass. He did it on his vacation time. I'll never forget it because he took me on one of his trips to the west coast. I think all of his people contributed because the pipe system was eventually built. He was always thinking of his village.[210]

---

[209] Interview with Spelson.
[210] Interview with Mary Kribales, Berwyn, Illinois, 24 September 1980.

Sentiment displayed by the immigrants toward Greece, whether it be assistance in a military struggle or sending money to villages for new construction, did not help their image in Chicago or other American cities. Many Americans resented those who displayed any patriotic feeling for their homeland after they settled in the United States. They were of the opinion that Greeks, and other ethnics, should concern themselves only for their newly adopted country and not the land of their origin. In many instances American resentment of this fact was most visible.

A Greek-American architect recalled the agony his grandfather experienced while working as a factory sweeper. He took the job in 1905 and saved as much money as he possibly could. He related very well with his fellow workers and the foreman but in 1908 he considered quitting and returning to his village in Greece to be with his family. When his co-workers learned of his intentions they stopped associating with him completely and never spoke to him again unless it was to denounce him for his views. Their displeasure soon evolved into hatred. He was labeled as a traitor by the laborers, and the foreman as well, until the day he left. It was their impression that he should not only refrain from returning to Greece but should denounce his country as well.[211]

Prejudice against Greeks and foreigners in general was considered to be more intense in the South where hatred of blacks and other minorities had been in existence for more than a century. Greeks in the cities and smaller towns felt a greater animosity toward them than their compatriots in the North and East had. Since many Greek businessmen in the South were successful, many Americans found it difficult to compete with them.

With the escalation of anti-foreign sentiment rising in the early 1920's many businessmen intimidated Greeks into selling their shops and property for less than their value. The activities of the Ku Klux Klan, and other groups, helped influence Greeks into forming a national organization for self-protection and establishing better relations with the non-Hellenic community.

---

[211] Interview with Ellis.

A small group of men in Atlanta took the initiative and formed the American Hellenic Educational Progressive Association on July 26, 1922. It sought to accomplish three major goals: 1) to promote and help establish better working relationships with the American public, 2) to assist in the adjustment of any occurrence that threatened peaceful relations between themselves and non-Greek groups, and 3) to assist the Greek social organization and religious parishes in eliminating their differences. With the formation of chapters throughout the United States, including Chicago, it became known as AHEPA.[212]

---

[212] Saloutos, The Greeks in America, p. 18.

CHAPTER VI

CONCLUSIONS

Courage is not the absence of fear. It is going forward with the face of fear.

Abraham Lincoln

To further our understanding of the Greek businessman in America, it is edifying to note that author Ivan Light, in his book entitled <u>Ethnic Enterprise in America</u>, discusses the means the Chinese, Japanese, and black American employed to confront the environmental barriers facing them. One of his significant findings, in the case of the Japanese and Chinese groups, focused on their dependence upon the various associations that were formed to financially assist members of their community in the opening of small businesses. These "rotating credit associations," known as <u>hui</u> among the Chinese and tanomoshi, or <u>mujin</u> among the Japanese, were traditional organizations which originated in the homeland and included only those who came from the particular region of their country which the organization represented.

They alleviated the difficulty in obtaining loans from prejudicial and untrustworthy American bankers and virtually guaranteed their members of the necessary capital needed to open a business. The importance of these groups in the Oriental-American business community was emphasized by Gor Yun Leong, author of <u>Chinatown Inside Out</u>, who stated that "without such societies, very few businesses could be started."[213]

Early Greek immigrants interested in opening small businesses, but whose reliability was unknown to the local financial community, also relied on compatriots from the same villages or regions in the homeland for assistance. Unlike the Orientals, however, any agreement concerning

---

[213] Ivan Light, <u>Ethnic Enterprise in America</u> (Berkeley: University of California Press, 1972), p. 27.

the lending of capital was limited to only two or three individuals and did not involve the pooling of money within large organizations.

Since the majority of the Greeks were profound individualists, they were unable to unify themselves into large business or financial associations. The only Greeks who made an effort toward unity were those who were threatened by outside competition. Most of the organizations formed for this purpose were only moderately successful. Thus, the cooperation and accomplishments which were characteristic of the Chinese hui and the Japanese mujin systems could not be realized in the Greek business community.

When comparing the long-term opportunities which existed in the Japanese, Chinese, and Greek business communities, the Greeks possessed certain advantages which inevitably made it easier for them to gain acceptance in the greater American community. Like most other Americans, the Greeks were white, Christian, and of European extraction. Once their ability to operate successful businesses was established, the procurement of funds from lending institutions was not difficult to obtain.

The black American small businessman also experienced many of the difficulties confronted by the Japanese and Chinese. His problems, however, were compounded by racial prejudice, deficiencies in formal education, and confinement in overcrowded ghettos. Most bankers realized that the development of business opportunities among blacks was extremely limited, and most of the loans granted to them were considered unfavorable by black business leaders. Several black-owned banks existed within large black communities, such as the Binga Bank in Chicago and others in New York and in the South, but most ended in failure.[214]

The initial confinement of the Greeks and other European immigrants to low-income, tenement neighborhoods, on the other hand, was temporary. Success in business, or in any other endeavor, was achievable through determination, hard work, and the establishment of attainable goals.

Despite the perpetual hardships confronted by the Greek businessman in Chicago during the period from 1900 to 1930, his determination and

---

[214] Ibid., p. 52.

fortitude to succeed surpassed any obstacle which threatened his existence. Coming from humble beginnings and without money, knowledge of the language, or an awareness of American business practices, he was able to emerge as one of the leading figures in the business community of Chicago and throughout the country.

His desire for wealth and financial independence was appropriately concomitant with the pride he envisaged in his national heritage and his ingenuity in adopting himself to a foreign and often hostile environment. When the Greek owner of a three-hundred-thousand-dollar-a- year clothing business was asked to what he attributed his success he replied: "Just hard work--that's all. Nobody can move you if you are right. Nobody can move you, no matter how strong they are."[215]

Perhaps the success of the Greek businessman is best illustrated in a story of unknown origin, but familiar to many individuals in the Greek community. It describes the experience of a poor immigrant from Greece who was told of a job-opening for a floor sweeper at a neighborhood bank. When he applied for it the bank manager rejected him because he didn't know how to write his name.

Several days later he went to the downtown market center, bought a load of fruits and vegetables and a small wagon and began roaming the streets as a peddler. After earning a considerable amount of money, he invested in his own business, which included a store and several trucks. When he went back to the bank to open an account, the bank manager, who had earlier rejected him, was amazed to learn of the financial success of the Greek and asked: "I wonder what you would have made of yourself if you only knew how to read and write?" The immigrant looked at him, smiled, and replied, "I would have been sweeping your floors."[216]

---

[215] June Namias, First Generation (Boston: Beacon Press, 1978), p. 29.
[216] Interview with Moraitis.

SELECTED BIBLIOGRAPHY

Primary Sources

"Advice to the Restaurants." Greek Press. 21 March 1935.

"American Association of Greek Restaurant-Keepers." Saloniki. 2 August 1924.

"The American is Misinformed." Greek Star. 7 October 1904.

"Andrew Karzas." Saloniki. 8 December 1922.

"Better Late Than Never." Saloniki. 23 October 1915.

"A Bloody Drama." Saloniki. 9 August 1913.

"Bootblacks Protective Union of Illinois." Chicago Greek Daily. 11 February 1928.

Burgess, Thomas. Greeks in America. Boston: Sherman, French, and Company, 1913.

"Candymakers Form Organization." Chicago Greek Daily. 18 August 1925.

"Chicago--Mecca of the Candy Business." Greek Star. 1 April 1904.

"The Confectioners." Saloniki. 3 June 1916.

"The Crusade." Greek Star. 1 March 1907.

"The DeMet's Store on Michigan Avenue." Saloniki. 13 December 1924.

Fairchild, Henry Pratt. "The Causes of Emigration from Greece." Yale Review 18 (August 1909).

Fairchild, Henry Pratt. Greek Immigration to the United States. New Haven: Yale University Press, 1911.

"The Flowers Sellers." Saloniki. 6 August 1927.

"Form Greek Enterprise." Saloniki. 2 February 1924.

"Grand Opening of a New Theatre." Saloniki. 20 September 1924.

"The Greek Merchants in Chicago." Saloniki. 25 January 1930.

"Greek Progress in Business." Saloniki. 16 May 1925.

"The Greek as a Restaurant Man." Greek Star. 14 November 1919.

"The Greek Restaurant in America." Chicago Greek Daily. 12 July 1929.

"Greek Trade is in Peril." Greek Press. 3 July 1929.

"The Guilty are Absolved." Saloniki. 9 October 1915.

"A Half-Million Dollar Lease." Chicago Greek Daily. 19 July 1926.

"Halsted Street Confectioners." Greek Press. 11 April 1935.

"How the Greeks Must Send Their Money to Greece." Greek Star. 3 December 1909.

"John Raklios and Company Leases New Store on Randolph Street." Saloniki. 13 March 1926.

"More About the Labor Meeting." Saloniki. 15 April 1916.

"Murder and Suicide." Saloniki. 26 April 1930.

"A New Commercial Success." Saloniki. 6 September 1924.

"New Restaurant Opened." Chicago Greek Daily. 30 April 1926.

"The New Restaurant of Raklios and Company." Saloniki. 27 February 1926.

Nickolson, George. Greek Directory of Chicago and Vicinity 1921-1922. Chicago: Nickolson Brothers, 1921.

"Progress Among Greeks." Saloniki. 5 July 1924.

"Progress and System." Loxias. 20 May 1909.

"The Restaurant Man." Saloniki. 17 December 1927.

"Successful Business." Saloniki. 17 February 1923.

"Temptation Candy Company." Saloniki. 18 June 1921.

"Temptation Chocolates." Saloniki. 17 May 1924.

"The Tragic History of the Greek-American Bank." Saloniki 2 October 1915.

"Trianon is Redecorated." Greek Press. 10 October 1935.

"Unification." Saloniki. 15 April 1916.

Secondary Sources

Adamic, Louis. A Nation of Nations. New York: Harper Brothers Publishers, 1944.

Chock, Phyllis Pease. "The Greek American Small Businessman: A Cultural Analysis." Journal of Anthropological Research 37 (Spring 1981).

City of Chicago. Department of Development and Planning. Historic City. The Settlement of Chicago. Chicago, Illinois, 1976.

Constant, Theodore N. "Employment and Business of the Greeks in the U.S." Athene VI (Winter 1945).

Constant, Theodore N. "Employment and Business of the Greeks in the U.S." Athene VII (Summer 1946).

Constant, Theodore N. "Employment and Business of the Greeks in the U.S." Athene VII (Autumn 1946).

Constant, Theodore N. "Employment and Business of the Greeks in the U.S." Athene VII (Winter, 1947).

Constant, Theodore N. "Greek Immigration and its Causes." Athene VIII (Spring 1947).

Fairchild, Henry Pratt. Race and Nationality. New York: The Ronald Press Company, 1947.

Fenton, Heike, and Hecker, Melvin. The Greeks in America 1528-1977. Dobbs Ferry, New York: Oceana Publications, 1978.

Light, Ivan. Ethnic Enterprise in America. Berkeley: University of California Press, 1972.

Miller, Wayne Charles. A Comprehensive Bibliography for the Study of American Minorities. New York: New York University Press, 1976.

Namias, June. First Generation. Boston: Beacon Press, 1978.

Saloutos, Theodore. The Greeks in America. A Student's Guide to Localized History. New York: Teachers College Press, Columbia University, 1967.

Saloutos, Theodore. The Greeks in the United States. Cambridge: Harvard University Press, 1964.

Selz, Thalia Cheronis. "The Switchboard." Chicago, October 1976.

Oral Sources

Andreou, Peter. Berwyn, Illinois. Interview, 18 March 1982.

Assimos, Constantine. Chicago, Illinois. Interview, 5 November 1981.

Bartsakis, Dimitri. Oak Park, Illinois. Interview, 23 September 1980.

Bell (Bambales), Peter. Oakbrook Terrace, Illinois. Interview 16 October, 1981.

Billions (Billionis), Chris. Stevensville, Michigan. Interview, 20 September 1981.

Ellis, Nicholas. Chicago, Illinois. Interview, 1 October 1980.

Kallas, James. Oak Park, Illinois. Interview, 12 September 1980.

Kribales, Mary. Berwyn, Illinois. Interview, 24 September 1980.

Mallason (Mallamis), Samuel. Berwyn, Illinois, Interview, 13 October 1980.

Milton (Miliotis), John. Bloomingdale, Illinois. Interview, 27 September 1981.

Moraitis, Mary. Forest Park, Illinois. Interview, 5 October 1981.

Rassogianis, George. Bloomingdale, Illinois. Interview, 27 September 1981.

Sedares, George. Forest Park, Illinois. Interview, 5 October 1981.

Skizas, Peter. Berwyn, Illinois. Interview, 19 September 1980.

Spear (Spiropoulos), Thomas. Berwyn, Illinois. Interview, 30 September 1981.

Spelson (Spirotopoulos), George. Oak Park, Illinois, Interview 30 September 1981.

Stoes, George. Stevensville, Michigan. Interview, 21 September 1981.

Stratigakes, Dimitri. Berwyn, Illinois. Interview, 28 September 1981.

Valos, Peter. Forest Park, Illinois. Interview, 19 September 1980.

Voltes, Peter. Oak Park, Illinois. Interview, 26 September 1980.

ABOUT THE AUTHOR

Alexander Rassogianis was born in Chicago, Illinois, to parents who emigrated from Sparta, Laconia, Greece. He received a bachelor's degree in history and political science from Elmhurst College and taught history in Chicago for more than fifteen years. He served as a compliance officer and investigated labor discrimination cases for the US Department of Labor for twenty years. Alex studied international relations abroad in Finland, and received a master's degree in history from the University of Wisconsin—Milwaukee in 1982. He is the author of *Return to Glenlord: Memories of Michigan Summers* and is currently writing a novel titled *Rainbow over Portland*. He lives in Berwyn, Illinois.

Made in the USA
Lexington, KY
15 February 2016